Alicia
EDITIONS

CHRISTMAS STORIES

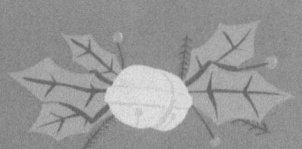

JACOB A. RIIS

CONTENTS

THE KID HANGS UP HIS STOCKING	1
IS THERE A SANTA CLAUS?	5
THE CROGANS' CHRISTMAS IN THE SNOWSHED	10
THE OLD TOWN	20
HIS CHRISTMAS GIFT	31
THE SNOW BABIES' CHRISTMAS	35
JACK'S SERMON	44
MERRY CHRISTMAS IN THE TENEMENTS	49
WHAT THE CHRISTMAS SUN SAW IN THE TENEMENTS	70
NIBSY'S CHRISTMAS	79
THE LITTLE DOLLAR'S CHRISTMAS JOURNEY	86
LITTLE WILL'S MESSAGE	94
THE BURGOMASTER'S CHRISTMAS	101

THE KID HANGS UP HIS STOCKING

The clock in the West Side Boys' Lodging-house ticked out the seconds of Christmas Eve as slowly and methodically as if six fat turkeys were not sizzling in the basement kitchen against the morrow's spread, and as if two-score boys were not racking their brains to guess what kind of pies would go with them. Out on the avenue the shop-keepers were barring doors and windows, and shouting "Merry Christmas!" to one another across the street as they hurried to get home. The drays ran over the pavement with muffled sounds; winter had set in with a heavy snow-storm. In the big hall the monotonous click of checkers on the board kept step with the clock. The smothered exclamations of the boys at some unexpected, bold stroke, and the scratching of a little fellow's pencil on a slate, trying to figure out how long it was yet till the big dinner, were the only sounds that broke the quiet of the room. The superintendent dozed behind his desk.

A door at the end of the hall creaked, and a head with a shock of weather-beaten hair was stuck cautiously through the opening.

"Tom!" it said in a stage-whisper. "Hi, Tom! Come up an' git on ter de lay of de Kid."

A bigger boy in a jumper, who had been lounging on two chairs by the group of checker players, sat up and looked toward the door. Something in the energetic toss of the head there aroused his instant curiosity, and he started across the room. After a brief whispered conference the door closed upon the two, and silence fell once more on the hall.

They had been gone but a little while when they came back in haste. The big boy shut the door softly behind him and set his back against it.

"Fellers," he said, "what d'ye t'ink? I'm blamed if de Kid ain't gone an' hung up his sock fer Chris'mas!"

The checkers dropped, and the pencil ceased scratching on the slate, in breathless suspense.

"Come up an' see," said Tom, briefly, and led the way.

The whole band followed on tiptoe. At the foot of the stairs their leader halted.

"Yer don't make no noise," he said, with a menacing gesture. "You, Savoy!"—to one in a patched shirt and with a mischievous twinkle,—"you don't come none o' yer monkey-shines. If you scare de Kid you'll get it in de neck, see!"

With this admonition they stole upstairs. In the last cot of the double tier of bunks a boy much smaller than the rest slept, snugly tucked in the blankets. A tangled curl of yellow hair strayed over his baby face. Hitched to the bedpost was a poor, worn little stocking, arranged with much care so that Santa Claus should have as little trouble in filling it as possible. The edge of a hole in the knee had been drawn together and tied with a string to prevent anything falling out. The boys looked on in amazed silence. Even Savoy was dumb.

Little Willie, or, as he was affectionately dubbed by the boys, "the Kid," was a waif who had drifted in among them some months before. Except that his mother was in the hospital, nothing was known about him, which was regular and according to the rule of the house. Not as much was known about most of its patrons; few of them knew more themselves, or cared to remember. Santa Claus had never been anything to them but a fake to make the colored supplements sell. The revelation of the Kid's simple faith struck them with a kind of awe. They sneaked quietly downstairs.

"Fellers," said Tom, when they were all together again in the big room, —by virtue of his length, which had given him the nickname of "Stretch," he was the speaker on all important occasions,—"ye seen it yerself. Santy Claus is a-comin' to this here joint to-night. I wouldn't 'a' believed it. I ain't never had no dealin's wid de ole guy. He kinder forgot I was around, I guess. But de Kid says he is a-comin' to-night, an' what de Kid says goes."

THE KID HANGS UP HIS STOCKING

Then he looked round expectantly. Two of the boys, "Gimpy" and Lem, were conferring aside in an undertone. Presently Gimpy, who limped, as his name indicated, spoke up.

"Lem says, says he——"

"Gimpy, you chump! you'll address de chairman," interrupted Tom, with severe dignity, "or you'll get yer jaw broke, if yer leg *is* short, see!"

"Cut it out, Stretch," was Gimpy's irreverent answer. "This here ain't no regular meetin', an' we ain't goin' to have none o' yer rot. Lem, he says, says he, let's break de bank an' fill de Kid's sock. He won't know but it wuz ole Santy done it."

A yell of approval greeted the suggestion. The chairman, bound to exercise the functions of office in season and out of season, while they lasted, thumped the table.

"It is regular motioned an' carried," he announced, "that we break de bank fer de Kid's Chris'mas. Come on, boys!"

The bank was run by the house, with the superintendent as paying teller. He had to be consulted, particularly as it was past banking hours; but the affair having been succinctly put before him by a committee, of which Lem and Gimpy and Stretch were the talking members, he readily consented to a reopening of business for a scrutiny of the various accounts which represented the boys' earnings at selling papers and blacking boots, minus the cost of their keep and of sundry surreptitious flings at "craps" in secret corners. The inquiry developed an available surplus of three dollars and fifty cents. Savoy alone had no account; the run of craps had recently gone heavily against him. But in consideration of the season, the house voted a credit of twenty-five cents to him. The announcement was received with cheers. There was an immediate rush for the store, which was delayed only a few minutes by the necessity of Gimpy and Lem stopping on the stairs to "thump" one another as the expression of their entire satisfaction.

The procession that returned to the lodging-house later on, after wearing out the patience of several belated storekeepers, might have been the very Santa's supply-train itself. It signalized its advent by a variety of discordant noises, which were smothered on the stairs by Stretch, with much personal violence, lest they wake the Kid out of season. With boots in hand and bated breath, the midnight band stole up to the dormitory and looked in. All was safe. The Kid was dreaming, and smiled in his sleep. The report roused a passing suspicion that he was faking, and Savarese was for pinching his toe to find out. As this would inevitably result in disclosure, Savarese and his proposal were scornfully sat upon. Gimpy supplied the popular explanation.

"He's a-dreamin' that Santy Claus has come," he said, carefully working a base-ball bat past the tender spot in the stocking.

"Hully Gee!" commented Shorty, balancing a drum with care on the end of it, "I'm thinkin' he ain't far out. Look's ef de hull shop'd come along."

It did when it was all in place. A trumpet and a gun that had made vain and perilous efforts to join the bat in the stocking leaned against the bed in expectant attitudes. A picture-book with a pink Bengal tiger and a green bear on the cover peeped over the pillow, and the bedposts and rail were festooned with candy and marbles in bags. An express-wagon with a high seat was stabled in the gangway. It carried a load of fir branches that left no doubt from whose livery it hailed. The last touch was supplied by Savoy in the shape of a monkey on a yellow stick, that was not in the official bill of lading.

"I swiped it fer de Kid," he said briefly in explanation.

When it was all done the boys turned in, but not to sleep. It was long past midnight before the deep and regular breathing from the beds proclaimed that the last had succumbed.

The early dawn was tinging the frosty window panes with red when from the Kid's cot there came a shriek that roused the house with a start of very genuine surprise.

"Hello!" shouted Stretch, sitting up with a jerk and rubbing his eyes. "Yes, sir! in a minute. Hello, Kid, what to——"

The Kid was standing barefooted in the passageway, with a base-ball bat in one hand and a trumpet and a pair of drumsticks in the other, viewing with shining eyes the wagon and its cargo, the gun and all the rest. From every cot necks were stretched, and grinning faces watched the show. In the excess of his joy the Kid let out a blast on the trumpet that fairly shook the building. As if it were a signal, the boys jumped out of bed and danced a breakdown about him in their shirt-tails, even Gimpy joining in.

"Holy Moses!" said Stretch, looking down, "if Santy Claus ain't been here an' forgot his hull kit, I'm blamed!"

IS THERE A SANTA CLAUS?

"Dear Mr. Riis:
   "A little chap of six on the Western frontier writes to us:
   "'Will you please tell me if there is a Santa Claus? Papa says not.'
   "Won't you answer him?"

That was the message that came to me from an editor last December just as I was going on a journey. Why he sent it to me I don't know. Perhaps it was because, when I was a little chap, my home was way up toward that white north where even the little boys ride in sleds behind reindeer, as they are the only horses they have. Perhaps it was because when I was a young lad I knew Hans Christian Andersen, who surely ought to know, and spoke his tongue. Perhaps it was both. I will ask the editor when I see him. Meanwhile, here was his letter, with Christmas right at the door, and, as I said, I was going on a journey.

I buttoned it up in my greatcoat along with a lot of other letters I didn't have time to read, and I thought as I went to the depot what a pity it was that my little friend's papa should have forgotten about Santa Claus. We big people do forget the strangest way, and then we haven't got a bit of a good time any more.

No Santa Claus! If you had asked that car full of people I would have liked to hear the answers they would have given you. No Santa Claus!

Why, there was scarce a man in the lot who didn't carry a bundle that looked as if it had just tumbled out of his sleigh. I felt of one slyly, and it was a boy's sled—a "flexible flyer," I know, because he left one at our house the Christmas before; and I distinctly heard the rattling of a pair of skates in that box in the next seat. They were all good-natured, every one, though the train was behind time—that is a sure sign of Christmas. The brakeman wore a piece of mistletoe in his cap and a broad grin on his face, and he said "Merry Christmas" in a way to make a man feel good all the rest of the day. No Santa Claus, is there? You just ask him!

And then the train rolled into the city under the big gray dome to which George Washington gave his name, and by-and-by I went through a doorway which all American boys would rather see than go to school a whole week, though they love their teacher dearly. It is true that last winter my own little lad told the kind man whose house it is that he would rather ride up and down in the elevator at the hotel, but that was because he was so very little at the time and didn't know things rightly, and, besides, it was his first experience with an elevator.

As I was saying, I went through the door into a beautiful white hall with lofty pillars, between which there were regular banks of holly with the red berries shining through, just as if it were out in the woods! And from behind one of them there came the merriest laugh you could ever think of. Do you think, now, it was that letter in my pocket that gave that guilty little throb against my heart when I heard it, or what could it have been? I hadn't even time to ask myself the question, for there stood my host all framed in holly, and with the heartiest handclasp.

"Come in," he said, and drew me after. "The coffee is waiting." And he beamed upon the table with the veriest Christmas face as he poured it out himself, one cup for his dear wife and one for me. The children—ah! you should have asked *them* if there was a Santa Claus!

And so we sat and talked, and I told my kind friends that my own dear old mother, whom I have not seen for years, was very, very sick in far-away Denmark and longing for her boy, and a mist came into my hostess's gentle eyes and she said, "Let us cable over and tell her how much we think of her," though she had never seen her. And it was no sooner said than done. In came a man with a writing-pad, and while we drank our coffee this message sped under the great stormy sea to the far-away country where the day was shading into evening already, though the sun was scarce two hours high in Washington:

IS THERE A SANTA CLAUS?

The White House.

Mrs. Riis, Ribe, Denmark:
Your son is breakfasting with us. We send you our love and sympathy.

Theodore and Edith Roosevelt.

For, you see, the house with the holly in the hall was the White House, and my host was the President of the United States. I have to tell it to you, or you might easily fall into the same error I came near falling into. I had to pinch myself to make sure the President was not Santa Claus himself. I felt that he had in that moment given me the very greatest Christmas gift any man ever received: my little mother's life. For really what ailed her was that she was very old, and I know that when she got the President's dispatch she must have become immediately ten years younger and got right out of bed. Don't you know mothers are that way when any one makes much of their boys? I think Santa Claus must have brought them all in the beginning—the mothers, I mean.

I would just give anything to see what happened in that old town that is full of blessed memories to me, when the telegraph ticked off that message. I will warrant the town hurried out, burgomaster, bishop, beadle and all, to do honor to my gentle old mother. No Santa Claus, eh? What was that, then, that spanned two oceans with a breath of love and cheer, I should like to know. Tell me that!

After the coffee we sat together in the President's office for a little while while he signed commissions, each and every one of which was just Santa Claus's gift to a grown-up boy who had been good in the year that was going; and before we parted the President had lifted with so many strokes of his pen clouds of sorrow and want that weighed heavily on homes I knew of to which Santa Claus had had hard work finding his way that Christmas.

It seemed to me as I went out of the door, where the big policeman touched his hat and wished me a Merry Christmas, that the sun never shone so brightly in May as it did then. I quite expected to see the crocuses and the jonquils, that make the White House garden so pretty, out in full bloom. They were not, I suppose, only because they are official flowers and have a proper respect for the calendar that runs Congress and the Executive Departments, too.

I stopped on the way down the avenue at Uncle Sam's paymaster's to see what he thought of it. And there he was, busy as could be, making ready for the coming of Santa Claus. No need of my asking any questions here. Men stood in line with bank-notes in their hands asking for gold, new gold-pieces, they said, most every one. The paymaster, who had a sprig of Christmas green fixed in his desk just like any other man, laughed and shook his head and said "Santa Claus?" and the men in the line laughed too and nodded and went away with their gold.

One man who went out just ahead of me I saw stoop over a poor woman on the corner and thrust something into her hand, then walk hastily away. It was I who caught the light in the woman's eye and the blessing upon her poor wan lips, and the grass seemed greener in the Treasury dooryard, and the sky bluer than it had been before, even on that bright day. Perhaps—well, never mind! if any one says anything to you about principles and giving alms, you tell him that Santa Claus takes care of the principles at Christmas, and not to be afraid. As for him, if you want to know, just ask the old woman on the Treasury corner.

And so, walking down that Avenue of Good-will, I came to my train again and went home. And when I had time to think it all over I remembered the letters in my pocket which I had not opened. I took them out and read them, and among them were two sent to me in trust for Santa Claus himself which I had to lay away with the editor's message until I got the dew rubbed off my spectacles. One was from a great banker, and it contained a check for a thousand dollars to help buy a home for some poor children of the East Side tenements in New York, where the chimneys are so small and mean that scarce even a letter will go up through them, so that ever so many little ones over there never get on Santa Claus's books at all.

The other letter was from a lonely old widow, almost as old as my dear mother in Denmark, and it contained a two-dollar bill. For years, she wrote, she had saved and saved, hoping some time to have five dollars, and then she would go with me to the homes of the very poor and be Santa Claus herself. "And wherever you decided it was right to leave a trifle, that should be the place where it would be left," read the letter. But now she was so old that she could no longer think of such a trip and so she sent the money she had saved. And I thought of a family in one of those tenements where father and mother are both lying ill, with a boy, who ought to be in school, fighting all alone to keep the wolf from the door, and winning the fight. I guess he has been too busy to send any message up the chimney, if indeed there is one in his house; but you ask him, right now, whether he thinks there is a Santa Claus or not.

No Santa Claus? Yes, my little man, there is a Santa Claus, thank God! Your father had just forgotten. The world would indeed be poor without one. It is true that he does not always wear a white beard and drive a reindeer team—not always, you know—but what does it matter? He is Santa Claus with the big, loving, Christmas heart, for all that; Santa Claus with the kind thoughts for every one that make children and grown-up people beam with happiness all day long. And shall I tell you a secret which I did not learn at the post-office, but it is true all the same—of how you can always be sure your letters go to him straight by the chimney route? It is this: send along with them a friendly thought for the boy you don't like: for Jack who punched you, or Jim who was mean to you. The meaner he was the harder do you resolve to make it up: not to bear him a grudge. That is the stamp for the letter to Santa. Nobody can stop it, not even a cross-draught in the chimney, when it has that on.

Because—don't you know, Santa Claus is the spirit of Christmas: and ever and ever so many years ago when the dear little Baby was born after whom we call Christmas, and was cradled in a manger out in the stable because there was not room in the inn, that Spirit came into the world to soften the hearts of men and make them love one another. Therefore, that is the mark of the Spirit to this day. Don't let anybody or anything rub it out. Then the rest doesn't matter. Let them tear Santa's white beard off at the Sunday-school festival and growl in his bearskin coat. These are only his disguises. The steps of the real Santa Claus you can trace all through the world as you have done here with me, and when you stand in the last of his tracks you will find the Blessed Babe of Bethlehem smiling a welcome to you. For then you will be home.

THE CROGANS' CHRISTMAS IN THE SNOWSHED

A storm was brewing in the mountains. The white glare of the earlier day had been supplanted by a dull gray, and the peaks that shut the winter landscape in were "smoking," sure harbinger of a blizzard already raging in the high Sierras. The pines above the Crogans' cabin stood like spectral sentinels in the failing light, their drooping branches heavy with the snow of many storms. Mrs. Tom Crogan sat at the window looking listlessly into the darkening day.

In the spring she had come with her husband from the little Minnesota town that was their home, full of hope and the joy of life. The mountains were beautiful then with wild flowers and the sweet smell of fragrant firs, and as she rocked her baby to sleep in their deep shadows she sang to him the songs her mother had crooned over her cradle in her tuneful Swedish tongue. Life then had seemed very fair, and the snowshed hardly a shadow across it. For to her life there were two sides: one that looked out upon the mountains and the trees and the wild things that stirred in God's beautiful world; the other the blind side that turned toward the darkness man had made in his fight to conquer that world. Tom Crogan was a dispatcher at a signal station in the great snowsheds that stretched forty miles or more up the slopes of the Sierras, plunging the road to the Land of Sunshine into hour-long gloom just when the jagged "saw-tooth" peaks, that give the range its name, came into sight.

THE CROGANS' CHRISTMAS IN THE SNOWSHED

Travelers knew them to their grief: a huge crawling thing of timber and stout planks—so it seemed as one caught fleeting glimpses of it in the brief escapes from its murky embrace—that followed the mountain up, hugging its side close as it rose farther and farther toward the summit. Hideous always, in winter buried often out of sight by the smashing avalanches Old Boreas hurled at the pigmy folk who dared challenge him in his own realm; but within the shelter of the snowsheds they laughed at his bluster, secure from harm, for then it served its appointed purpose.

The Crogans' house fronted or backed—whichever way one chose to look at it—upon the shed. Tom's office, where the telegraph ticker was always talking of men and things in the desert sands to the east, or in the orange groves over the Divide, never saw the sunshine it told of. It burrowed in perpetual gloom. Nine times a day trains full of travelers, who peered curiously at the signalmen with their lanterns and at Tom as so many human moles burrowing in the mountain, came and went, and took the world of men with them, yawning as they departed at the prospect of more miles of night. At odd intervals long freight trains lingered, awaiting orders, and lent a more human touch. For the engineer had time to swap yarns with Tom, and the brakemen looked in to chuck the baby under the chin and to predict, when their smudge faces frightened him, that he would grow up to be as fine a railroader as his father: his yell was as good as a whistle to "down brakes." Even a wandering hobo once in a while showed his face from behind the truck on which he was stealing a ride 'cross country, and grimaced at Mrs. Tom, safe in the belief that she would not give him away. And she didn't.

But now the winter had come with the heavy snows that seemed never to end. She could not venture out upon the mountain where the pines stood buried many feet deep. In truth there was no getting out. Her life side was banked up, as it were, to stay so till spring came again. As she sat watching the great white waste that sloped upward toward the lowering sky she counted the months: two, three, four—five, probably, or six, to wait. For this was Christmas, and the winter was but fairly under way. Five months! The winters were hard enough on the plains, but the loneliness of these mountains! What glad visiting and holiday-making were going on now in her old home among kindred and friends! There it was truly a season of kindliness and good cheer; they had brought their old Norse Yule with them across the seas. She choked back a sob as she stirred the cradle with her foot. For Tom's sake she would be brave. But no letter nor word had come from the East, and this their first Christmas away from home!

There was a man's step on the stairs from the office, and Tom Crogan put his head through the doorway.

"Got a bite for a hungry man?" he asked, blinking a bit at the white light from without.

The baby woke up and gurgled. Tom waved the towel at him, drying his face at the sink, and hugged his wife as she passed.

"Storm coming," he said, glancing out at the weather and listening to the soughing of the wind in the pines.

"Nothing else here," she replied, setting the table; "nothing this long while, and, oh, Tom!"—she set down the plate and went over to him—"no word from home, and this is Christmas Eve. Nothing even for the baby."

He patted her back affectionately, and cheered her after the manner of a man.

"Trains all late, the snow is that deep, more particular in the East, they say. Mail might not come through for a week. Baby don't know the difference so long as he is warm. And coal we've got a-plenty."

"Then it will be New Year's," she pursued her own thoughts drearily. Tom was not a good comforter just then.

He ate like a tired man, in silence. "Special on the line," he said, as he stirred the sugar in his coffee. "When the road opens up she'll follow right on the Overland."

"Some o' your rich folks, most like, going for a holiday on the Coast," she commented without interest. Tom nodded. She gave the stove lid an impatient twist.

"Little they know," she said bitterly, "or care either, how we live up here in the sheds. They'd oughter take their turn at it a while. There's the Wrights with Jim laid up since he broke his leg at the time o' the wreck, and can't seem to get no strength. And the Coulsons with their old mother in this grippin' cold, an' all the sickness they've had, an' he laid off, though he wasn't to blame, an' you know it, Tom. If it hadn't been for you what would 'a' come to the Overland runnin' straight for that wrecked freight with full head o' steam——"

Tom looked up good-humoredly and pushed back his plate.

"Why, Mary! what's come over you? I only done what I was there to do —and they took notice all right. Don't you remember the Company wrote and thanked me for bein' spry?"

"Thanked you!" contemptuously. "What good is that? Here we be, an' like to stay till——You can come up if you want to."

The invitation was extended, ungraciously enough, to a knot of men clustered about the steps. They trooped in, a gang of snow-shovelers fresh from their fight with the big drifts, and stood about the stove, the cold breath of outdoors in their looks and voices. Their talk was of their work just finished. The road was clear, but for how long? And they flapped their frozen mittens toward the window through which the snow could be seen already beginning to fall in large, ominous flakes. The Special was discussed with eager interest. No one knew who it was—an unusual thing. Generally words came along the line giving the news, but there had been no warning of this one.

"Mebbe it's the President inspectin'," ventured one of the crew.

"I tank it bane some o' dem Wall Street fellers on one big bust," threw in a husky Swede.

In the laugh that followed this sally the ticker was heard faintly clicking out a message in the office below.

Tom listened. "Overland three hours late," he said, and added with a glance outside as he made ready to go: "like as not they'll be later'n that; they won't keep Christmas on the Coast this while."

The snow-shovelers trailed out after Tom with many a fog-horn salute of Merry Christmas to his wife and to the baby. The words, well meant, jarred harshly upon Mrs. Crogan.

Merry Christmas! It sounded in her ear almost like a taunt. When they were gone she stood at the window, struggling with a sense of such bitter desolation as she had never known till then. The snow fell thick now, and was whirled across the hillside in fitful gusts. In the gathering darkness trees and rocks were losing shape and color; nothing was left but the white cold, the thought of which chilled her to the marrow. Through the blast the howl of a lone wolf came over the ridge, and she remembered the story of Donner Lake, just beyond, and the party of immigrants who starved to death in the forties, shut in by such a winter as this. There were ugly tales on the mountain of things done there, which men told under their breath when the great storms thundered through the cañons and all were safe within. She had heard the crew of the rotary say that there was as much as ten feet of snow on some of the levels already, and the winter only well begun. Without knowing it she fell to counting the months to spring again: two, three, four, five! With a convulsive shudder she caught up the child and fled to the darkest corner of the room. Crouching there by the fire her grief and bitterness found vent in a flood of rebellious tears.

Down in his dark coop Tom Crogan, listening to a distant roar and the quickening rhythm of the rails, knew that the Overland was coming. Presently it shot out from behind the shoulder of the mountain. Ordinarily it passed swiftly enough, but to-day it slowed up and came to a stop at the station. The conductor hurried into the office and held an anxious consultation with Tom, who shook his head decisively. If the storm kept up there would be no getting out that night. The cut over at the lake that had just been cleared was filling up again sure with the wind blowing from the north. There was nothing to do but wait, anyhow until they knew for certain. The conductor agreed with bad grace, and the rotary was started up the road to reconnoiter. The train discharged its weary and worried passengers, who walked up and down the dark cavern to stretch their legs, glancing indifferently at the little office where the telegraph kept up its intermittent chatter.

Suddenly it clicked out a loud warning: "Special on way. Clear the track."

Tom rapped on his window and gave quick orders. The men hurried to carry them out.

"Not far she'll go," they grinned as they set the switch and made all safe. At the turn half a mile below the red eye of the locomotive gleamed already in the dusk. In a few minutes it pulled in with a shriek of its whistle that woke the echoes of the hills far and near, and stood panting in a cloud of steam. Trackmen and signalmen craned their necks to see the mysterious stranger. Even Mrs. Tom had dried her tears and came out to look at the despised bigbugs from the East, rebellion yet in her homesick heart.

The news that the "Big Boss" might be on board had spread to the passenger train, and crowds flocked from the sleepers, curious to get a glimpse of the railroad magnate who had made such a stir in the land. His power was so great that common talk credited him with being stronger than Congress and the courts combined. The newspapers recorded all his doings as it did the President's, but with this difference, that while everybody knew all about the Man in the White House, few if any seemed to know anything real about the railroad man's private life. In the popular estimation he was a veritable Sphinx. At his country home in the East he had bought up the land for five miles around—even the highways—to keep intruders out. Here now was an unexpected chance, and the travelers crowded up to get a look at him.

But they saw no luxurious private car with frock-coated officials and liveried servants. An every-day engine with three express cars in tow stood upon the track, and baggagemen in blue overalls yelled for hand-trucks, and hustled out boxes and crates consigned to "The agent at Shawnee." Yet it was not an every-day train nor an ordinary crew; for all of them, conductor, brakemen, engineer and fireman, wore holly in their caps and broad grins on their faces. The locomotive flew two white flags with the words "Merry Christmas" in red letters, and across the cars a strip of canvas was strung their whole length, with the legend "The Christmas Train" in capitals a foot long. Even in the gloom of the snowshed it shone out, plain to read.

Tom in his office rubbed his eyes for another and better look when the conductor of the Special, pushing his way through the wondering crowds, flung open the door.

"Here's yer docyments," he said, slapping down a paper, "and the orders are that ye're to see they gets 'em."

Tom Crogan took up the paper as if dazed, and looked at the entries without in the least understanding what it all meant. He did not see the jam of railroad men and passengers who had crowded into the office on the heels of the conductor until they filled it to the doors. Neither did he notice that his wife had come with them and was standing beside him looking as mystified as he. Mechanically he read out the items in the waybill, while the conductor checked them off with many a wink at the crowd. What nightmare was this? Had some delirious Santa Claus invaded the office of the Union Pacific Railroad, and turned it into a toy shop and dry-goods bazar combined, with a shake of his reindeer bells? Or was it a huge, wretched, misbegotten joke? Surely stranger bill of lading never went over the line, or over any railroad line before. This was what he read:

"Crate of fat turkeys, one for every family on the station (their names followed).

"One ditto of red apples.

"One ditto of oranges, to be similarly apportioned.

"For Tom Crogan, one meerschaum pipe.

"For James Wright, lately injured in the service and not yet recovered, a box of books, and allowance of full pay during disability. Ordered to report at Sacramento until fully restored.

"For John Coulson, Christmas gifts, including a warm flannel wrapper for his old mother; also notice of back pay allowed since suspension, with full restoration to place and pay.

"For Mrs. Thomas Crogan, not on the official payroll, but whom the Company takes this opportunity to thank for assistance rendered her husband on a recent occasion, one dress pattern, with the wishes of the Superintendent's office for a very Merry Christmas.

"For Master Thomas Crogan, not yet on the official payroll, being under age, a box of toys, including rubber ball and sheep, doll and Noah's ark, with the compliments of the Company for having chosen so able a railroad man for his father.

"For Master Thomas Crogan, as a token of regard from passengers on the Overland of November 18, one rocking-horse, crated."

"Oh, Tom!"—Mrs. Crogan caught her breath with a gasp—"and he not a year old!"

Tom looked up to find the room full of people laughing at him and at her, but there was hearty, happy good-will in the laugh, and Mrs. Tom was laughing back.

The conductor got up to go, but checked himself abruptly. "If I didn't come near to forget," he said and reached for his pocket. "Here, Tom, this is for you from the Superintendent. If it ain't a secret read it aloud."

The message was brief:

Thomas Crogan, Esq.,
   Agent and Dispatcher at Shawnee Station:
   The compliments of the season and of the Superintendent's office to you. Have a Merry Christmas, Tom, up in your shed, for we want you down on the Coast after New Year's.

FRANK ALDEN,
Superintendent.

Tom looked up with a smile. He had got his bearings at last. There was no doubt about that signature. His eyes met his wife's, brimming with sudden joy. The dream of her life was made real.

The railroad men raised a cheer in which there was a note of regret, for Tom was a prime favorite with them all, and crowded up to shake hands. The passengers followed suit, ready to join in, yet mystified still. But now, when they heard from the conductor of the Special how Tom by quick action had saved the Overland, the very train they were on, from running into a wrecked freight two months before, many of them remembered the story of it—how Tom, being left alone when everybody else lost his head in the smashup, had sprinted down the track with torpedoes, while his wife set the switch and waved the signal lantern, and had just caught the Limited around the curve, and how narrow had been the escape from a great disaster. And their quick sympathy went out to the young couple up in the lonely heights, who a few moments before had been less to them than the inert thing of iron and steel that was panting on the track outside like a huge monster after a hard run.

When it was learned that both trains were stalled, perhaps for all night, the recollection that it was Christmas Eve gave sudden direction to their sympathies. Since friends on the Coast must wait they would have their Christmas where they were, if it were in a snowshed. In less time than any one could have made a formal motion the trainful of excited passengers, just now so disgruntled, resolved itself into a committee of arrangements to which were added both the train crews.

A young balsam from the mountainside made its appearance, no one knew exactly how, and in a trice it shone with a wealth of candles and toys at which the baby, struggling up to a sitting posture in his cradle, looked with wide-eyed wonder. The Crogans' modest living-room was made festive with holly and evergreen and transformed into a joyous dining-room before Mrs. Tom could edge in a word of protest. All the memories of her cherished Yule surged in upon her as the room filled with the smell of roast turkey and mince pie and what not of good cheer, borne in by a procession of white-clad waiters who formed a living chain between the dining-car and the station. When in the wake of them the veritable rocking-horse, hastily unpacked, was led in by a hysterical darky, and pranced and pawed its way across the floor, its reins jingling with silver bells, Thomas Crogan, Junior, considered it, sitting bolt upright, one long minute, sighed and, overwhelmed by such magnificence, went calmly to sleep. It was too much for one Christmas Eve, and he not a year old.

When as many as could crowd in were seated with Tom Crogan and his wife—the conductors and engineers of the two trains representing the road—the clergyman in the party arose to remind them all that they were far from home and friends, keeping Christmas in the mountain wilderness.

"But," he said, "though a continent separates us we meet with them all here to-night before the face of Him who came as a helpless Babe to the world of sin and selfishness, and brought peace and good-will to men." And he read to them how "It came to pass in those days, that there went out a decree from Cæsar Augustus, that all the world should be taxed," and the story of the Child that is old, yet will be ever new while the world stands.

In the reverent hush that had fallen upon the company a tenor voice rose clear and sweet in the old hymn:

> *"It came upon the midnight clear*
> *That glorious song of old."*

When the lines were reached:

> *"Still through the cloven skies they come*
> *With peaceful wings unfurl'd,"*

many of the passengers joined in and sang the verse to the end. The familiar words seemed to come with a comforting message to every one in the little cabin.

In the excitement they had all forgotten the weather. Unseen by every one the moon had come out and shone clear in an almost cloudless sky. The storm was over. A joyful toot of the rotary's whistle, as dinner neared its end, announced its return with the welcome news that the road was open once more.

With many hearty handshakes, and wishes for happy years to come, the unexpected Christmas party broke up. But there was yet a small ceremony left. It was performed by a committee of three of the Overland passengers who had friends or kin on board the train Tom Crogan had saved. They had quietly circulated among the rest, and now, with the conductor shouting "All aboard!" they put an envelope into Tom's hand, with the brief directions "for moving expenses," and jumped on their car as the engine blew its last warning whistle and the airbrakes wheezed their farewell.

Tom opened it and saw five crisp twenty-dollar bills tucked neatly inside.

THE CROGANS' CHRISTMAS IN THE SNOWSHED

The Limited pulled out on the stroke of midnight, with cheering passengers on every step and in every window. Tom and his wife stood upon the step of the little station and waved their handkerchiefs as long as the bull's-eye on the last car was in sight. When it was gone and they were left with the snowshed and the Special breathing sleepily on its siding she laid her head on his shoulder. A rush of repentant tears welled up and mingled with the happiness in her voice.

"Oh, Tom!" she said. "Did ye ever know the like of it? I am fair sorry to leave the old shed."

THE OLD TOWN

I do not know how the forty years I have been away have dealt with "Jule-nissen," the Christmas elf of my childhood. He was pretty old then, gray and bent, and there were signs that his time was nearly over. So it may be that they have laid him away. I shall find out when I go over there next time. When I was a boy we never sat down to our Christmas Eve dinner until a bowl of rice and milk had been taken up to the attic, where he lived with the marten and its young, and kept an eye upon the house—saw that everything ran smoothly. I never met him myself, but I know the house-cat must have done so. No doubt they were well acquainted; for when in the morning I went in for the bowl, there it was, quite dry and licked clean, and the cat purring in the corner. So, being there all night, he must have seen and likely talked with him.

I suspect, as I said, that they have not treated my Nisse fairly in these matter-of-fact days that have come upon us, not altogether for our own good, I fear. I am not even certain that they were quite serious about him then, though to my mind that was very unreasonable. But then there is nothing so unreasonable to a child as the cold reason of the grown-ups. However, if they have gone back on him, I know where to find him yet. Only last Christmas when I talked of him to the tenement-house mothers in my Henry Street Neighborhood House,[1]—all of them from the ever faithful isle,—I saw their eyes light up with the glad smile of recognition, and half a dozen called out excitedly, "The Little People! the Leprecawn ye mean, we know him well," and they were not more pleased than I to find that we had an old friend in common. For the Nisse, or the Leprecawn, call him whichever you like, was a friend indeed to those who loved kindness and peace. If there was a house in which contention ruled, either he would have nothing to do with it, like the stork that built its nest on the roof, or else he paid the tenants back in their own coin, playing all kinds of tricks upon them and making it very uncomfortable. I suppose it was this trait that gave people, when they began to reason so much about things, the notion that he was really the wraith, as it were, of their own disposition, which was not so at all. I remember the story told of one man who quarrelled with everybody, and in consequence had a very troublesome Nisse in the house that provoked him to the point of moving away; which he did. But as the load of furniture was going down the street, with its owner hugging himself in glee at the thought that he had stolen a march on the Nisse, the little fellow poked his head out of the load and nodded to him, "We are moving to-day." At which naturally he flew into a great rage. But then, that was just a story.

The Nisse was of the family, as you see, very much of it, and certainly not to be classed with the cattle. Yet they were his special concern; he kept them quiet, and saw to it, when the stableman forgot, that they were properly bedded and cleaned and fed. He was very well known to the hands about the farm, and they said that he looked just like a little old man, all in gray and with a pointed red nightcap and long gray beard. He was always civilly treated, as he surely deserved to be, but Christmas was his great holiday, when he became part of it, indeed, and was made much of. So, for that matter, was everything that lived under the husbandman's roof, or within reach of it. The farmer always set a lighted candle in his window on Christmas Eve, to guide the lonesome wanderer to a hospitable hearth. The very sparrows that burrowed in the straw thatch, and did it no good, were not forgotten. A sheaf of rye was set out in the snow for them, so that on that night at least they should have shelter and warmth unchallenged, and plenty to eat. At all other times we were permitted to raid their nests and help ourselves to a sparrow roast, which was by long odds the greatest treat we had. Thirty or forty of them, dug out of any old thatch roof by the light of the stable lantern and stuffed into Ane's long stocking, which we had borrowed for a game-bag, made a meal for the whole family, each sparrow a fat mouthful. Ane was the cook, and I am very certain that her pot-roast of sparrow would pass muster at any Fifth Avenue restaurant as the finest dish of reed-birds that ever was. However, at Christmas their sheaf was their sanctuary, and no one as much as squinted at them. Only last winter when Christmas found me stranded in a little Michigan town, wandering disconsolate about the streets, I came across such a sheaf raised on a pole in a dooryard, and I knew at once that one of my people lived in that house and kept Yule in the old way. So I felt as if I were not quite a stranger.

All the animals knew perfectly well that the holiday had come, and kept it in their way. The watch-dog was unchained. In the midnight hour on the Holy Eve the cattle stood up in their stalls and bowed out of respect and reverence for Him who was laid in a manger when there was no room in the inn, and in that hour speech was given them, and they talked together. Claus, our neighbor's man, had seen and heard it, and every Christmas Eve I meant fully to go and be there when it happened; but always long before that I had been led away to bed, a very sleepy boy, with all my toys hugged tight, and when I woke up the daylight shone through the frosted window-panes, and they were blowing good morning from the church tower; it would be a whole year before another Christmas. So I vowed, with a sigh at having neglected a really sacred observance, that I would be there sure on the next Christmas Eve. But it was always so, every year, and perhaps it was just as well, for Claus said that it might go ill with the one who listened, if the cows found him out.

Blowing in the Yule from the grim old tower that had stood eight hundred years against the blasts of the North Sea was one of the customs of the Old Town that abide, however it fares with the Nisse; that I know. At sun-up, while yet the people were at breakfast, the town band climbed the many steep ladders to the top of the tower, and up there, in fair weather or foul,—and sometimes it blew great guns from the wintry sea, —they played four old hymns, one to each corner of the compass, so that no one was forgotten. They always began with Luther's sturdy challenge, "A Mighty Fortress is our God," while down below we listened devoutly. There was something both weird and beautiful about those far-away strains in the early morning light of the northern winter, something that was not of earth and that suggested to my child's imagination the angels' song on far Judean hills. Even now, after all these years, the memory of it does that. It could not have been because the music was so rare, for the band was made up of small storekeepers and artisans who thus turned an honest penny on festive occasions. Incongruously enough, I think, the official town mourner who bade people to funerals was one of them. It was like the burghers' guard, the colonel of which—we thought him at least a general, because of the huge brass sword he trailed when he marched at the head of his men—was the town tailor, a very small but very martial man. But whether or no, it was beautiful. I have never heard music since that so moved me. When the last strain died away came the big bells with their deep voices that sang far out over field and heath, and our Yule was fairly under way.

A whole fortnight we kept it. Real Christmas was from Little Christmas Eve, which was the night before the Holy Eve proper, till New Year. Then there was a week of supplementary festivities before things slipped back into their wonted groove. That was the time of parties and balls. The great ball of the year was on the day after Christmas. Second Christmas Day we called it, when all the quality attended at the clubhouse, where the Amtmand and the Burgomaster, the Bishop and the Rector of the Latin School, did the honors and received the people. That was the grandest of the town functions. The school ball, late in autumn, was the jolliest, for then the boys invited each the girl he liked best, and the older people were guests and outsiders, so to speak. The Latin School, still the "Cathedral School," was as old as the Domkirke itself, and when it took the stage it was easily first while it lasted. The Yule ball, though it was a rather more formal affair, for all that was neither stiff nor tiresome; nothing was in the Old Town; there was too much genuine kindness for that. And that it was the recognized occasion when matches were made by enterprising mammas, or by the young themselves, and when engagements were declared and discussed as the great news of the day. We heard of all those things afterward and thought a great fuss was being made over nothing much. For when a young couple were declared engaged, that meant that there was no more fun to be out of them. They were given, after that, to go mooning about by themselves and to chasing us children away when we ran across them; until they happily returned to their senses, got married, and became reasonable human beings once more.

When we had been sent to bed on the great night, Father and Mother went away in their Sunday very best, and we knew they would not return until two o'clock in the morning, a fact which alone invested the occasion with unwonted gravity, for the Old Town kept early hours. At ten o'clock, when the watchman droned his sleepy lay, absurdly warning the people to

> *Be quick and bright,*
> *Watch fire and light,*
> *Our clock it has struck ten,*

it was ordinarily tucked in and asleep. But that night we lay awake a long time listening to the muffled sound of heavy wheels in the snow rolling unceasingly past, and trying to picture to ourselves the grandeur they conveyed. Every carriage in the town was then in use and doing overtime. I think there were as many as four.

When we were not dancing or playing games, we literally ate our way through the two holiday weeks. Pastry by the mile did we eat, and general indigestion brooded over the town when it emerged into the white light of the new year. At any rate it ought to have done so. It is a prime article of faith with the Danes to this day that for any one to go out of a friend's house, or of anybody's house, in the Christmas season without partaking of its cheer, is to "bear away their Yule," which no one must do on any account. Every house was a bakery from the middle of December until Christmas Eve, and oh! the quantities of cakes we ate, and such cakes! We were sixteen normally, in our home, and Mother mixed the dough for her cakes in a veritable horse-trough kept for that exclusive purpose. As much as a sack of flour went in, I guess, and gallons of molasses and whatever else went to the mixing. For weeks there had been long and anxious speculations as to "what Father would do," and gloomy conferences between him and Mother over the state of the family pocket-book, which was never plethoric; but at last the joyful message ran through the house from attic to kitchen that the appropriation had been made, "even for citron," which meant throwing all care to the winds. The thrill of it, when we children stood by and saw the generous avalanche going into the trough! What would not come out of it! The whole family turned to and helped make the cakes and cut the "pepper-nuts," which were little squares of spiced cake-dough we played cards for and stuffed our pockets with, gnawing them incessantly. Talk about eating between meals: ours was a continuous performance for two solid weeks. The pepper-nuts were the real staple of Christmas to us children. We paid forfeits with them in the game of scratch-nose (jackstraws), when the fellow fishing for his straw stirred the others and had his nose scratched with the little file in the bunch as extra penalty; in "Under which tree lies my pig?" in which the pig was a pepper-nut, the fingers of the closed hands the trees; and in Black Peter. In this last the loser had his nose blackened with the snuff from the candle until advancing civilization substituted a burnt cork. Christmas without pepper-nuts would have been a hollow mockery indeed. We rolled the dough in long strings like slender eels and then cut it, a little on the bias. They were good, those nuts, when baked brown. I wish I had some now.

It all stood for the universal desire that in the joyous season everybody be made glad. I know that in the Old Town no one went hungry or cold during the holidays, if indeed any one ever did. Every one gave of what he had, and no one was afraid of pauperizing anybody by his gifts, for they were given gladly and in love, and that makes all the difference—did then and does now. At Christmas it is perfectly safe to let our scientific principles go and just remember the Lord's command that we love one another. I subscribe to them all with perfect loyalty, and try to practise them till Christmas week comes in with its holly and the smell of balsam and fir, and the memories of childhood in the Old Town; then—well, anyway, it is only a little while. New Year and the long cold winter come soon enough.

Christmas Eve was, of course, the great and blessed time. That was the one night in the year when in the gray old Domkirke services were held by candle-light. A myriad wax candles twinkled in the gloom, but did not dispel it. It lingered under the great arches where the voice of the venerable minister, the responses of the congregation, and above it all the boyish treble of the choir billowed and strove, now dreamily with the memories of ages past, now sharply, tossed from angle to corner in the stone walls, and again in long thunderous echoes, sweeping all before it on the triumphant strains of the organ, like a victorious army with banners crowding through the halls of time. So it sounded to me, as sleep gently tugged at my eyelids. The air grew heavy with the smell of evergreens and of burning wax, and as the thunder of war drew farther and farther away, in the shadow of the great pillars stirred the phantoms of mailed knights whose names were hewn in the grave-stones there. We youngsters clung to the skirts of Mother as we went out and the great doors fell to behind us. And yet those Christmas Eves, with Mother's gentle eyes forever inseparable from them, and with the glad cries of Merry Christmas ringing all about, have left a touch of sweet peace in my heart which all the years have not effaced, nor ever will.

At home the great dinner of the year was waiting for us; roast goose stuffed with apples and prunes, rice pudding with cinnamon and sugar on it, and a great staring butter eye in the middle. The pudding was to lay the ground-work with, and it was served in deep soup-plates. It was the dish the Nisse came in on, and the cat. On New Year's Eve both these were left out; but to make up for it an almond was slipped into the "gröd," and whoever found it in his plate got a present. It was no device to make people "fletch," but it served the purpose admirably. At Christmas we had doughnuts after the goose, big and stout and good. However I managed it, I don't know, but it is a tradition in the family, and I remember it well, that I once ate thirteen on top of the big dinner. Evidently I was having a good time. Dinner was, if not the chief end of man, at least an item in his make-up, and a big one.[2]

When it had had time to settle and all the kitchen work was done, Father took his seat at the end of the long table, with all the household gathered about, the servants included and the baby without fail, and read the story of The Child: "And it came to pass in those days," while Mother hushed the baby. Then we sang together "A Child is Born in Bethlehem," which was the simplest of our hymns, and also the one we children loved best, for it told of how in heaven we were to walk to church

> On sky-blue carpets, star-bedeckt,

which was a great comfort. Children love beautiful things, and we had few of them. The great and precious treasure in our house was the rag carpet in the spare room which we were allowed to enter only on festive occasions such as Christmas. It had an orange streak in it which I can see to this day. Whenever I come across one that even remotely suggests it, it gives me yet a kind of solemn feeling. We had no piano,—that was a luxury in those days,—and Father was not a singer, but he led on bravely with his tremulous bass and we all joined in, Ane the cook and Maria the housemaid furtively wiping their eyes with their aprons, for they were good and pious folk and this was their Christmas service. So we sang the ten verses to end, with their refrain "Hallelujah! hallelujah," that always seemed to me to open the very gates of Yule.

And it did, literally; for when the last hallelujah died away the door of the spare room was flung wide and there stood the Christmas tree, all shining lights, and the baby was borne in, wide-eyed, to be the first, as was proper; for was not this The Child's holiday? Unconsciously we all gave way to those who were nearest Him, who had most recently come from His presence and were therefore in closest touch with the spirit of the holiday. So, when we joined hands and danced around the tree, Father held the baby, and we laughed and were happy as the little one crowed his joy and stretched his tiny arms toward the light.

Light and shadow, joy and sorrow, go hand in hand in the world. While we danced and made merry, there was one near for whom

Christmas was but grief and loss. Out in the white fields he went from farm to farm, a solitary wanderer, the folklore had it, looking for plough or harrow on which to rest his weary limbs. It was the Wandering Jew, to whom this hope was given, that, if on that night of all in the year he could find some tool used in honest toil over which the sign of the cross had not been made, his wanderings would be at an end and the curse depart from him, to cleave thence-forward to the luckless farmer.[3] He never found what he sought in my time. The thrifty husbandman had been over his field on the eve of the holiday with a watchful eye to his coming. When the bell in the distant church tower struck the midnight hour, belated travellers heard his sorrowful wail as he fled over the heath and vanished.

When Ansgarius preached the White Christ to the vikings of the North, so runs the legend of the Christmas tree, the Lord sent His three messengers, Faith, Hope, and Love, to help light the first tree. Seeking one that should be high as hope, wide as love, and that bore the sign of the cross on every bough, they chose the balsam fir, which best of all the trees in the forest met the requirements. Perhaps that is a good reason why there clings about the Christmas tree in my old home that which has preserved it from being swept along in the flood of senseless luxury that has swamped so many things in our money-mad day. At least so it was then. Every time I see a tree studded with electric lights, garlands of tinsel-gold festooning every branch, and hung with the hundred costly knicknacks the storekeepers invent year by year "to make trade," until the tree itself disappears entirely under its burden, I have a feeling what a fraud has been practised on the kindly spirit of Yule. Wax candles are the only real thing for a Christmas tree, candles of *wax* that mingle their perfume with that of the burning fir, not the by-product of some coal-oil or other abomination. What if the boughs do catch fire; they can be watched, and too many candles are tawdry, anyhow. Also, red apples, oranges, and old-fashioned cornucopias made of colored paper, and made at home, look a hundred times better and fitter in the green; and so do drums and toy trumpets and waldhorns, and a rocking-horse reined up in front that need not have cost forty dollars, or anything like it.

I am thinking of one, or rather two, a little piebald team with a wooden seat between, for which Mother certainly did not give over seventy-five cents at the store, that as "Belcher and Mamie"—the names were bestowed on the beasts at sight by Kate, aged three, who bossed the play-room—gave a generation of romping children more happiness than all the expensive railroads and trolley-cars and steam-engines that are considered indispensable to keeping Christmas nowadays. And the Noah's Ark with Noah and his wife and all the animals that went two by two—ah, well! I haven't set out to preach a sermon on extravagance that makes no one happier, but I wish—The legend makes me think of the holly that grew in our Danish woods. We called it Christ-thorn, for to us it was of that the crown of thorns was made with which the cruel soldiers mocked our Saviour, and the red berries were the drops of blood that fell from His anguished brow. Therefore the holly was a sacred tree, and to this day the woods in which I find it seem to me like the forest where the Christmas roses bloomed in the night when the Lord was born, different from all other woods, and better.

Mistletoe was rare in Denmark. There was known to be but one oak in all the land on which it grew. But that did not discourage the young. We had our kissing games which gave the boys and girls their chance to choose sides, and in the Christmas season they went on right merrily. There was rarely a night that did not bring the children together under some roof or other. They say that kissing goes by favor, but we had not arrived at that point yet, though we had our preferences. In the game of Post Office, for instance, he was a bold boy who would dare call out the girl he really liked, to get the letter that was supposed to be awaiting her. You could tell for a dead certainty who was his choice by watching whom he studiously avoided asking for. I have a very vivid recollection of having once really dared with sudden desperation, and of the defiant flushed face, framed in angry curls, that confronted me in the hall, the painful silence while we each stood looking the other way and heard our playmates tittering behind the closed door,—for well they knew,—and her indignant stride as she went back to her seat unkissed, with me trailing behind, feeling like a very sheepish boy, and no doubt looking the part.

The Old Year went out with much such a racket as we make nowadays, but of quite a different kind. We did not blow the New Year in, we "smashed" it in. When it was dark on New Year's Eve, we stole out with all the cracked and damaged crockery of the year that had been hoarded for the purpose and, hieing ourselves to some favorite neighbor's door, broke our pots against it. Then we ran, but not very far or very fast, for it was part of the game that if one was caught at it, he was to be taken in and treated to hot doughnuts. The smashing was a mark of favor, and the citizen who had most pots broken against his door was the most popular man in town. When I was in the Latin School, a cranky burgomaster, whose door had been freshly painted, gave orders to the watchmen to stop it and gave them an unhappy night, for they were hard put to it to find a way it was safe to look, with the streets full of the best citizens in town, and their wives and daughters, sneaking singly by with bulging coats on their way to salute a friend. That was when our mothers—those who were not out smashing in New Year—came out strong, after the fashion of mothers. They baked more doughnuts than ever that night, and beckoned the watchman in to the treat; and there he sat, blissfully deaf while the street rang with the thunderous salvos of our raids; until it was discovered that the burgomaster himself was on patrol, when there was a sudden rush from kitchen doors and a great scurrying through streets that grew strangely silent.

The town had its revenge, however. The burgomaster, returning home in the midnight hour, stumbled in his gate over a discarded Christmas tree hung full of old boots and many black and sooty pots that went down around him with great smash in the upset, so that his family came running out in alarm to find him sprawling in the midst of the biggest celebration of all. His dignity suffered a shock which he never got over quite. But it killed the New Year's fun, too. For he was really a good fellow, and then he was the burgomaster, and chief of police to boot. I suspect the fact was that the pot smashing had run its course. Perhaps the supply of pots was giving out; we began to use tinware more about that time. That was the end of it, anyhow.

We boys got square, too, with the watchmen. We knew their habit of stowing themselves away in the stage-coach that stood in the marketplace when they had cried the hour at ten o'clock, and we caught them napping there one dark night when we were coming home from a party. The stage had doors that locked on the outside. We slammed them shut and ran the conveyance, with them in it wildly gesticulating from the windows, through the main street of the town, amid the cheers of the citizens whom the racket aroused from their slumbers. We were safe enough. The watchmen were not anxious to catch us, maddened as they were by our prank, and they were careful not to report us either. I chuckled at that exploit more than once when, in years long after, I went the rounds of the midnight streets with Haroun-al-Roosevelt, as they called New York's Police Commissioner, to find his patrolmen sleeping soundly on their posts when they should have been catching thieves. Human nature, police human nature, anyhow, is not so different, after all, in the old world and in the new.

THE OLD TOWN

With Twelfth Night our Yule came to an end. In that night, if a girl would know her fate, she must go to bed walking backward and throw a shoe over her left shoulder, or hide it under her pillow, I forget which, perhaps both, and say aloud a verse that prayed the Three Holy Kings to show her the man

> *Whose table I must set,*
> *Whose bed I must spread,*
> *Whose name I must bear,*
> *Whose bride I must be.*

The man who appeared to her in her sleep was to be her husband. There was no escape from it, and consequently she did not try. He was her Christmas gift, and she took him for better or for worse. Let us hope that the Nisse played her no scurvy trick, and that it was for better always.

---

1. The Jacob A. Riis Neighborhood Settlement, New York.
2. The reader who is not afraid of dyspepsia by suggestion may consider the following Christmas bill of fare which obtained among the peasants east of the Old Town: On a large trencher a layer of pork and ribs, on top of that a nest of fat sausages, in which sat a roast duck.
3. An unromantic variation of this was the belief that the farmer who left his plough out on Christmas would get a drubbing from his wife within a twelvemonth. I hope whoever held to that got what he richly deserved.

HIS CHRISTMAS GIFT

"The prisoner will stand," droned out the clerk in the Court of General Sessions. "Filippo Portoghese, you are convicted of assault with intent to kill. Have you anything to say why sentence should not be passed upon you?"

A sallow man with a hopeless look in his heavy eyes rose slowly in his seat and stood facing the judge. There was a pause in the hum and bustle of the court as men turned to watch the prisoner. He did not look like a man who would take a neighbor's life, and yet so nearly had he done so, of set purpose it had been abundantly proved, that his victim would carry the disfiguring scar of the bullet to the end of his life, and only by what seemed an almost miraculous chance had escaped death. The story as told by witnesses and substantially uncontradicted was this:

Portoghese and Vito Ammella, whom he shot, were neighbors under the same roof. Ammella kept the grocery on the ground floor. Portoghese lived upstairs in the tenement. He was a prosperous, peaceful man, with a family of bright children, with whom he romped and played happily when home from his barber shop. The Black Hand fixed its evil eye upon the family group and saw its chance. One day a letter came demanding a thousand dollars. Portoghese put it aside with the comment that this was New York, not Italy. Other letters followed, threatening harm to his children. Portoghese paid no attention, but his wife worried. One day the baby, little Vito, was missing, and in hysterics she ran to her husband's shop crying that the Black Hand had stolen the child.

The barber hurried home and sought high and low. At last he came upon the child sitting on Ammella's doorstep; he had wandered away and brought up at the grocery; asked where he had been, the child pointed to the store. Portoghese flew in and demanded to know what Ammella was doing with his boy. The grocer was in a bad humor, and swore at him. There was an altercation, and Ammella attacked the barber with a broom, beating him and driving him away from his door. Black with anger, Portoghese ran to his room and returned with a revolver. In the fight that followed he shot Ammella through the head.

He was arrested and thrown into jail. In the hospital the grocer hovered between life and death for many weeks. Portoghese lay in the Tombs awaiting trial for more than a year, believing still that he was the victim of a Black Hand conspiracy. When at last the trial came on, his savings were all gone, and of the once prosperous and happy man only a shadow was left. He sat in the court-room and listened in moody silence to the witnesses who told how he had unjustly suspected and nearly murdered his friend. He was speedily convicted, and the day of his sentence was fixed for Christmas Eve. It was certain that it would go hard with him. The Italians were too prone to shoot and stab, said the newspapers, and the judges were showing no mercy.

The witnesses had told the truth, but there were some things they did not know and that did not get into the evidence. The prisoner's wife was ill from grief and want; their savings of years gone to lawyer's fees, they were on the verge of starvation. The children were hungry. With the bells ringing in the glad holiday, they were facing bitter homelessness in the winter streets, for the rent was in arrears and the landlord would not wait. And "Papa" away now for the second Christmas, and maybe for many yet to come! Ten, the lawyer and jury had said: this was New York, not Italy. In the Tombs the prisoner said it over to himself, bitterly. He had thought only of defending his own.

So now he stood looking the judge and the jury in the face, yet hardly seeing them. He saw only the prison gates opening for him, and the gray walls shutting him out from his wife and little ones for—how many Christmases was it? One, two, three—he fell to counting them over mentally and did not hear when his lawyer whispered and nudged him with his elbow. The clerk repeated his question, but he merely shook his head. What should he have to say? Had he not said it to these men and they did not believe him? About little Vito who was lost, and his wife who cried her eyes out because of the Black Hand letters. He——

There was a step behind him, and a voice he knew spoke. It was the voice of Ammella, his neighbor, with whom he used to be friends before —before that day.

"Please, your Honor, let this man go! It is Christmas, and we should have no unkind thoughts. I have none against Filippo here, and I ask you to let him go."

It grew very still in the court-room as he spoke and paused for an answer. Lawyers looked up from their briefs in astonishment. The jurymen in the box leaned forward and regarded the convicted man and his victim with rapt attention. Such a plea had not been heard in that place before. Portoghese stood mute; the voice sounded strange and far away to him. He felt a hand upon his shoulder that was the hand of a friend, and shifted his feet uncertainly, but made no response. The gray-haired judge regarded the two gravely but kindly.

"Your wish comes from a kind heart," he said. "But this man has been convicted. The law must be obeyed. There is nothing in it that allows us to let a guilty man go free."

The jurymen whispered together and one of them arose.

"Your Honor," he said, "a higher law than any made by man came into the world at Christmas—that we love one another. These men would obey it. Will you not let them? The jury pray as one man that you let mercy go before justice on this Holy Eve."

A smile lit up Judge O'Sullivan's face. "Filippo Portoghese," he said, "you are a very fortunate man. The law bids me send you to prison for ten years, and but for a miraculous chance would have condemned you to death. But the man you maimed for life pleads for you, and the jury that convicted you begs that you go free. The Court remembers what you have suffered and it knows the plight of your family, upon whom the heaviest burden of your punishment would fall. Go, then, to your home. And to you, gentlemen, a happy holiday such as you have given him and his! This court stands adjourned."

The voice of the crier was lost in a storm of applause. The jury rose to their feet and cheered judge, complainant, and defendant. Portoghese, who had stood as one dazed, raised eyes that brimmed with tears to the bench and to his old neighbor. He understood at last. Ammella threw his arm around him and kissed him on both cheeks, his disfigured face beaming with joy. One of the jurymen, a Jew, put his hand impulsively in

HIS CHRISTMAS GIFT

his pocket, emptied it into his hat, and passed the hat to his neighbor. All the others followed his example. The court officer dropped in half a dollar as he stuffed its contents into the happy Italian's pocket. "For little Vito," he said, and shook his hand.

"Ah!" said the foreman of the jury, looking after the reunited friends leaving the court-room arm in arm; "it is good to live in New York. A merry Christmas to you, Judge!"

THE SNOW BABIES' CHRISTMAS

"All aboard for Coney Island!" The gates of the bridge train slammed, the whistle shrieked, and the cars rolled out past rows of houses that grew smaller and lower to Jim's wondering eyes, until they quite disappeared beneath the track. He felt himself launching forth above the world of men, and presently he saw, deep down below, the broad stream with ships and ferry-boats and craft going different ways, just like the tracks and traffic in a big, wide street; only so far away was it all that the pennant on the topmast of a vessel passing directly under the train seemed as if it did not belong to his world at all. Jim followed the white foam in the wake of the sloop with fascinated stare, until a puffing tug bustled across its track and wiped it out. Then he settled back in his seat with a sigh that had been pent up within him twenty long, wondering minutes since he limped down the Subway at Twenty-third Street. It was his first journey abroad.

Jim had never been to the Brooklyn Bridge before. It is doubtful if he had ever heard of it. If he had, it was as of something so distant, so unreal, as to have been quite within the realm of fairyland, had his life experience included fairies. It had not. Jim's frail craft had been launched in Little Italy, half a dozen miles or more up-town, and there it had been moored, its rovings being limited at the outset by babyhood and the tenement, and later on by the wreck that had made of him a castaway for life. A mysterious something had attacked one of Jim's ankles, and, despite ointments and lotions prescribed by the wise women of the tenement, had eaten into the bone and stayed there. At nine the lad was a cripple with one leg shorter than the other by two or three inches, with a stepmother, a squalling baby to mind for his daily task, hard words and kicks for his wage; for Jim was an unprofitable investment, promising no returns, but, rather, constant worry and outlay. The outlook was not the most cheering in the world.

But, happily, Jim was little concerned about things to come. He lived in the day that is, fighting his way as he could with a leg and a half and a nickname,—"Gimpy" they called him for his limp,—and getting out of it what a fellow so handicapped could. After all, there were compensations. When the gang scattered before the cop, it did not occur to him to lay any of the blame to Gimpy, though the little lad with the pinched face and sharp eyes had, in fact, done scouting duty most craftily. It was partly in acknowledgment of such services, partly as a concession to his sharper wits, that Gimpy was tacitly allowed a seat in the councils of the Cave Gang, though in the far "kid" corner. He limped through their campaigns with them, learned to swim by "dropping off the dock" at the end of the street into the swirling tide, and once nearly lost his life when one of the bigger boys dared him to run through an election bonfire like his able-bodied comrades. Gimpy started to do it at once, but stumbled and fell, and was all but burned to death before the other boys could pull him out. This act of bravado earned him full membership in the gang, despite his tender years; and, indeed, it is doubtful if in all that region there was a lad of his age as tough and loveless as Gimpy. The one affection of his barren life was the baby that made it slavery by day. But, somehow, there was that in its chubby foot groping for him in its baby sleep, or in the little round head pillowed on his shoulder, that more than made up for it all.

Ill luck was surely Gimpy's portion. It was not a month after he had returned to the haunts of the gang, a battle-scarred veteran now since his encounter with the bonfire, when "the Society's" officers held up the huckster's wagon from which he was crying potatoes with his thin, shrill voice, which somehow seemed to convey the note of pain that was the prevailing strain of his life. They made Gimpy a prisoner, limp, stick, and all. The inquiry that ensued as to his years and home setting, the while Gimpy was undergoing the incredible experience of being washed and fed regularly three times a day, set in motion the train of events that was at present hurrying him toward Coney Island in midwinter, with a snow-storm draping the land in white far and near, as the train sped seaward.

He gasped as he reviewed the hurrying event of the week: the visit of the doctor from Sea Breeze, who had scrutinized his ankle as if he expected to find some of the swag of the last raid hidden somewhere about it. Gimpy never took his eyes off him during the examination. No word or cry escaped him when it hurt most, but his bright, furtive eyes never left the doctor or lost one of his movements. "Just like a weasel caught in a trap," said the doctor, speaking of his charge afterward.

But when it was over, he clapped Gimpy on the shoulder and said it was all right. He was sure he could help.

"Have him at the Subway to-morrow at twelve," was his parting direction; and Gimpy had gone to bed to dream that he was being dragged down the stone stairs by three helmeted men, to be fed to a monster breathing fire and smoke at the foot of the stairs.

Now his wondering journey was disturbed by a cheery voice beside him. "Well, bub, ever see that before?" and the doctor pointed to the gray ocean line dead ahead. Gimpy had not seen it, but he knew well enough what it was.

"It's the river," he said, "that I cross when I go to Italy."

"Right!" and his companion held out a helping hand as the train pulled up at the end of the journey. "Now let's see how we can navigate."

And, indeed, there was need of seeing about it. Right from the step of the train the snow lay deep, a pathless waste burying street and sidewalk out of sight, blocking the closed and barred gate of Dreamland, of radiant summer memory, and stalling the myriad hobby-horses of shows that slept their long winter sleep. Not a whinny came on the sharp salt breeze. The strident voice of the carpenter's saw and the rat-tat-tat of his hammer alone bore witness that there was life somewhere in the white desert. The doctor looked in dismay at Gimpy's brace and high shoe, and shook his head.

"He never can do it. Hello, there!" An express wagon had come into view around the corner of the shed. "Here's a job for you." And before he could have said Jack Robinson, Gimpy felt himself hoisted bodily into the wagon and deposited there like any express package. From somewhere a longish something that proved to be a Christmas-tree, very much wrapped and swathed about, came to keep him company. The doctor climbed up by the driver, and they were off. Gimpy recalled with a dull sense of impending events in which for once he had no shaping hand, as he rubbed his ears where the bitter blast pinched, that to-morrow was Christmas.

THE SNOW BABIES' CHRISTMAS

A strange group was that which gathered about the supper-table at Sea Breeze that night. It would have been sufficiently odd to any one anywhere; but to Gimpy, washed, in clean, comfortable raiment, with his bad foot set in a firm bandage, and for once no longer sore with the pain that had racked his frame from babyhood, it seemed so unreal that once or twice he pinched himself covertly to see if he were really awake. They came weakly stumping with sticks and crutches and on club feet, the lame and the halt, the children of sorrow and suffering from the city slums, and stood leaning on crutch or chair for support while they sang their simple grace; but neither in their clear childish voices nor yet in the faces that were turned toward Gimpy in friendly scrutiny as the last comer, was there trace of pain. Their cheeks were ruddy and their eyes bright with the health of outdoors, and when they sang about the "Frog in the Pond," in response to a spontaneous demand, laughter bubbled over around the table. Gimpy, sizing his fellow-boarders up according to the standards of the gang, with the mental conclusion that he "could lick the bunch," felt a warm little hand worming its way into his, and, looking into a pair of trustful baby eyes, choked with a sudden reminiscent pang, but smiled back at his friend and felt suddenly at home. Little Ellen, with the pervading affections, had added him to her family of brothers. What honors were in store for him in that relation Gimpy never guessed. Ellen left no one out. When summer came again she enlarged the family further by adopting the President of the United States as her papa, when he came visiting to Sea Breeze; and by rights Gimpy should have achieved a pull such as would have turned the boss of his ward green with envy.

It appeared speedily that something unusual was on foot. There was a subdued excitement among the children which his experience diagnosed at first flush as the symptoms of a raid. But the fact that in all the waste of snow on the way over he had seen nothing rising to the apparent dignity of candy-shop or grocery-store made him dismiss the notion as untenable. Presently unfamiliar doings developed. The children who could write scribbled notes on odd sheets of paper, which the nurses burned in the fireplace with solemn incantations. Something in the locked dining-room was an object of pointed interest. Things were going on there, and expeditions to penetrate the mystery were organized at brief intervals, and as often headed off by watchful nurses.

When, finally, the children were gotten upstairs and undressed, from the headposts of each of thirty-six beds there swung a little stocking, limp and yawning with mute appeal. Gimpy had "caught on" by this time: it

THE SNOW BABIES' CHRISTMAS

was a wishing-bee, and old Santa Claus was supposed to fill the stockings with what each had most desired. The consultation over, baby George had let him into the game. Baby George did not know enough to do his own wishing, and the thirty-five took it in hand while he was being put to bed.

"Let's wish for some little dresses for him," said big Mariano, who was the baby's champion and court of last resort; "that's what he needs." And it was done. Gimpy smiled a little disdainfully at the credulity of the "kids." The Santa Claus fake was out of date a long while in his tenement. But he voted for baby George's dresses, all the same, and even went to the length of recording his own wish for a good baseball bat. Gimpy was coming on.

Going to bed in that queer place fairly "stumped" Gimpy. "Peelin'" had been the simplest of processes in Little Italy. Here they pulled a fellow's clothes off only to put on another lot, heavier every way, with sweater and hood and flannel socks and mittens to boot, as if the boy were bound for a tussle with the storm outside rather than for his own warm bed. And so, in fact, he was. For no sooner had he been tucked under the blankets, warm and snug, than the nurses threw open all the windows, every one, and let the gale from without surge in and through as it listed; and so they left them. Gimpy shivered as he felt the frosty breath of the ocean nipping his nose, and crept under the blanket for shelter. But presently he looked up and saw the other boys snoozing happily like so many little Eskimos equipped for the North Pole, and decided to keep them company. For a while he lay thinking of the strange things that had happened that day, since his descent into the Subway. If the gang could see him now. But it seemed far away, with all his past life—farther than the river with the ships deep down below. Out there upon the dark waters, in the storm, were they sailing now, and all the lights of the city swallowed up in gloom? Presently he heard through it all the train roaring far off in the Subway and many hurrying feet on the stairs. The iron gates clanked—and he fell asleep with the song of the sea for his lullaby. Mother Nature had gathered her child to her bosom, and the slum had lost in the battle for a life.

The clock had not struck two when from the biggest boy's bed in the corner there came in a clear, strong alto the strains of "Ring, ring, happy bells!" and from every room childish voices chimed in. The nurses hurried to stop the chorus with the message that it was yet five hours to daylight. They were up, trimming the tree in the dining-room; at the last moment the crushing announcement had been made that the candy had been forgotten, and a midnight expedition had set out for the city through the storm to procure it. A semblance of order was restored, but cat naps ruled after that, till, at day-break, a gleeful shout from Ellen's bed proclaimed that Santa Claus had been there, in very truth, and had left a dolly in her stocking. It was the signal for such an uproar as had not been heard on that beach since Port Arthur fell for the last time upon its defenders three months before. From thirty-six stockings came forth a veritable army of tops, balls, wooden animals of unknown pedigree, oranges, music-boxes, and cunning little pocket-books, each with a shining silver quarter in, love-tokens of one in the great city whose heart must have been light with happy dreams in that hour. Gimpy drew forth from his stocking a very able-bodied baseball bat and considered it with a stunned look. Santa Claus was a fake, but the bat—there was no denying that, and he *had* wished for one the very last thing before he fell asleep!

Daylight struggled still with a heavy snow-squall when the signal was given for the carol "Christmas time has come again," and the march down to breakfast. That march! On the third step the carol was forgotten and the band broke into one long cheer that was kept up till the door of the dining-room was reached. At the first glimpse within, baby George's wail rose loud and grievous: "My chair! my chair!" But it died in a shriek of joy as he saw what it was that had taken its place. There stood the Christmas-tree, one mass of shining candles, and silver and gold, and angels with wings, and wondrous things of colored paper all over it from top to bottom. Gimpy's eyes sparkled at the sight, skeptic though he was at nine; and in the depths of his soul he came over, then and there, to Santa Claus, to abide forever—only he did not know it yet.

To make the children eat any breakfast, with three gay sleds waiting to take the girls out in the snow, was no easy matter; but it was done at last, and they swarmed forth for a holiday in the open. All days are spent in the open at Sea Breeze,—even the school is a tent,—and very cold weather only shortens the brief school hour; but this day was to be given over to play altogether. Winter it was "for fair," but never was coasting enjoyed on New England hills as these sledding journeys on the sands where the surf beat in with crash of thunder. The sea itself had joined in making Christmas for its little friends. The day before, a regiment of crabs had come ashore and surrendered to the cook at Sea Breeze. Christmas morn found the children's "floor"—they called the stretch of clean, hard sand between high-water mark and the surf-line by that name—filled with gorgeous shells and pebbles, and strange fishes left there by the tide

THE SNOW BABIES' CHRISTMAS

overnight. The fair-weather friends who turn their backs upon old ocean with the first rude blasts of autumn little know what wonderful surprises it keeps for those who stand by it in good and in evil report.

When the very biggest turkey that ever strutted in barnyard was discovered steaming in the middle of the dinner-table and the report went round in whispers that ice-cream had been seen carried in pails, and when, in response to a pull at the bell, Matron Thomsen ushered in a squad of smiling mamas and papas to help eat the dinner, even Gimpy gave in to the general joy, and avowed that Christmas was "bully." Perhaps his acceptance of the fact was made easier by a hasty survey of the group of papas and mamas, which assured him that his own were not among them. A fleeting glimpse of the baby, deserted and disconsolate, brought the old pucker to his brow for a passing moment; but just then big Fred set off a snapper at his very ear, and thrusting a pea-green fool's-cap upon his head, pushed him into the roistering procession that hobbled round and round the table, cheering fit to burst. And the babies that had been brought down from their cribs, strapped, because their backs were crooked, in the frames that look so cruel and are so kind, lifted up their feeble voices as they watched the show with shining eyes. Little baby Helen, who could only smile and wave "by-by" with one fat hand, piped in with her tiny voice, "Here I is!" It was all she knew, and she gave that with a right good will, which is as much as one can ask of anybody, even of a snow baby.

If there were still lacking a last link to rivet Gimpy's loyalty to his new home for good and all, he himself supplied it when the band gathered under the leafless trees—for Sea Breeze has a grove in summer, the only one on the island—and whiled away the afternoon making a "park" in the snow, with sea-shells for curbing and boundary stones. When it was all but completed, Gimpy, with an inspiration that then and there installed him leader, gave it the finishing touch by drawing a policeman on the corner with a club, and a sign, "Keep off the grass." Together they gave it the air of reality and the true local color that made them feel, one and all, that now indeed they were at home.

Toward evening a snow-storm blew in from the sea, but instead of scurrying for shelter, the little Eskimos joined the doctor in hauling wood for a big bonfire on the beach. There, while the surf beat upon the shore hardly a dozen steps away, and the storm whirled the snow-clouds in weird drifts over sea and land, they drew near the fire, and heard the doctor tell stories that seemed to come right out of the darkness and grow real while they listened. Dr. Wallace is a southerner and lived his childhood with Br'er Rabbit and Mr. Fox, and they saw them plainly gamboling in the firelight as the story went on. For the doctor knows boys and loves them, that is how.

No one would have guessed that they were cripples, every one of that rugged band that sat down around the Christmas supper-table, rosy-cheeked and jolly—cripples condemned, but for Sea Breeze, to lives of misery and pain, most of them to an early death and suffering to others. For their enemy was that foe of mankind, the White Plague, that for thousands of years has taken tithe and toll of the ignorance and greed and selfishness of man, which sometimes we call with one name—the slum. Gimpy never would have dreamed that the tenement held no worse threat for the baby he yearned for than himself, with his crippled foot, when he was there. These things you could not have told even the fathers and mothers; or if you had, no one there but the doctor and the nurses would have believed you. They knew only too well. But two things you could make out, with no trouble at all, by the lamplight: one, that they were one and all on the homeward stretch to health and vigor—Gimpy himself was a different lad from the one who had crept shivering to bed the night before; and this other, that they were the sleepiest crew of youngsters ever got together. Before they had finished the first verse of "America" as their good night, standing up like little men, half of them were down and asleep with their heads pillowed upon their arms. And so Miss Brass, the head nurse, gathered them in and off to bed.

"And now, boys," she said as they were being tucked in, "your prayers." And of those who were awake each said his own: Willie his "Now I lay me," Mariano his "Ave," but little Bent from the Eastside tenement wailed that he didn't have any. Bent was a newcomer like Gimpy.

"Then," said six-year-old Morris, resolutely,—he also was a Jew,—"I learn him mine vat my fader tol' me." And getting into Bent's crib, he crept under the blanket with his little comrade. Gimpy saw them reverently pull their worsted caps down over their heads, and presently their tiny voices whispered together, in the jargon of the East Side, their petition to the Father of all, who looked lovingly down through the storm upon his children of many folds.

The last prayer was said, and all was still. Through the peaceful breathing of the boys all about him, Gimpy, alone wakeful, heard the deep bass of the troubled sea. The storm had blown over. Through the open windows shone the eternal stars, as on that night in the Judean hills when shepherds herded their flocks and

"The angels of the Lord came down."

He did not know. He was not thinking of angels; none had ever come to his slum. But a great peace came over him and filled his child-soul. It may be that the nurse saw it shining in his eyes and thought it fever. It may be that she, too, was thinking in that holy hour. She bent over him and laid a soothing hand upon his brow.

"You must sleep now," she said.

Something that was not of the tenement, something vital, with which his old life had no concern, welled up in Gimpy at the touch. He caught her hand and held it.

"I will if you will sit here," he said. He could not help it.

"Why, Jimmy?" She stroked back his shock of stubborn hair. Something glistened on her eyelashes as she looked at the forlorn little face on the pillow. How should Gimpy know that he was at that moment leading another struggling soul by the hand toward the light that never dies?

"'Cause," he gulped hard, but finished manfully—"'cause I love you."

Gimpy had learned the lesson of Christmas,

"And glory shone around."

JACK'S SERMON

Jack sat on the front porch in a very bad humor indeed. That was in itself something unusual enough to portend trouble; for ordinarily Jack was a philosopher well persuaded that, upon the whole, this was a very good world and Deacon Pratt's porch the centre of it on week-days. On Sundays it was transferred to the village church, and on these days Jack received there with the family. If the truth were told, it would probably have been found that Jack conceived the services to be some sort of function specially designed to do him honor at proper intervals, for he always received an extra petting on these occasions. He sat in the pew beside the deacon through the sermon as decorously as befitted a dog come to years of discretion long since, and wagged his tail in a friendly manner when the minister came down and patted him on the head after the benediction. Outside he met the Sunday-school children on their own ground, and on their own terms. Jack, if he didn't have blood, had sense, which for working purposes is quite as good, if not so common. The girls gave him candy and called him Jack Sprat. His joyous bark could be heard long after church as he romped with the boys by the creek on the way home. It was even suspected that on certain Sabbaths they had enjoyed a furtive cross-country run together; but by tacit consent the village overlooked it and put it down to the dog. Jack was privileged and not to blame. There was certainly something, from the children's point of view, also, in favor of Jack's conception of Sunday.

JACK'S SERMON

On week-day nights there were the church meetings of one kind and another, for which Deacon Pratt's house was always the place, not counting the sociables which Jack attended with unfailing regularity. They would not, any of them, have been quite regular without Jack. Indeed, many a question of grave church polity had been settled only after it had been submitted to and passed upon in meeting by Jack. "Is not that so, Jack?" was a favorite clincher to arguments which, it was felt, had won over his master. And Jack's groping paw cemented a treaty of good-will and mutual concession that had helped the village church over more than one hard place. For there were hard heads and stubborn wills in it as there are in other churches; and Deacon Pratt, for all he was a just man, was set on having his way.

And now all this was changed. What had come over the town Jack couldn't make out, but that it was something serious nobody was needed to tell him. Folks he used to meet at the gate, going to the trains of mornings, on neighborly terms, hurried past him without as much as a look. Deacon Jones, who gave him ginger-snaps out of the pantry-crock as a special bribe for a hand-shake, had even put out his foot to kick him, actually kick him, when he waylaid him at the corner that morning. The whole week there had not been as much as a visitor at the house, and what with Christmas in town—Jack knew the signs well enough; they meant raisins and goodies that came only when they burned candles on trees in the church—it was enough to make any dog cross. To top it all, his mistress must come down sick, worried into it all, as like as not, he had heard the doctor say. If Jack's thoughts could have been put into words as he sat on the porch looking moodily over the road, they would doubtless have taken something like this shape, that it was a pity that men didn't have the sense of dogs, but would bear grudges and make themselves and their betters unhappy. And in the village there would have been more than one to agree with him secretly.

Jack wouldn't have been any the wiser had he been told that the trouble that had come to town was that of all things most worrisome, a church quarrel. What was it about and how did it come? I doubt if any of the men and women who strove in meeting for principle and conscience with might and main, and said mean things about each other out of meeting, could have explained it. I know they all would have explained it differently, and so added fuel to the fire that was hot enough already. In fact, that was what had happened the night before Jack encountered his special friend, Deacon Jones, and it was in virtue of his master's share in it that he had bestowed the memorable kick upon him. Deacon Pratt was the valiant leader of the opposing faction.

To the general stress of mind the holiday had but added another cause of irritation. Could Jack have understood the ethics of men he would have known that it strangely happens that:

> "Forgiveness to the injured does belong,
> But they ne'er pardon who have done the wrong,"

and that everybody in a church quarrel having injured everybody else within reach for conscience sake, the season of good-will and even the illness of that good woman, the wife of Deacon Pratt, admittedly from worry over the trouble, practically put a settlement of it out of the question. But being only a dog he did not understand. He could only sulk; and as this went well enough with things as they were in general, it proved that Jack was, as was well known, a very intelligent dog.

He had yet to give another proof of it, that very day, by preaching to the divided congregation its Christmas sermon, a sermon that is to this day remembered in Brownville; but of that neither they nor he, sitting there on the stoop nursing his grievances, had at that time any warning.

It was Christmas Eve. Since the early Lutherans settled there, away back in the last century, it had been the custom in the village to celebrate the Holy Eve with a special service and a Christmas tree; and preparations had been going forward for it all the afternoon. It was noticeable that the fighting in the congregation in no wise interfered with the observance of the established forms of worship; rather, it seemed to lend a keener edge to them. It was only the spirit that suffered. Jack, surveying the road from the porch, saw baskets and covered trays carried by, and knew their contents. He had watched the big Christmas tree going down on the grocer's sled, and his experience plus his nose supplied the rest. As the lights came out one by one after twilight, he stirred uneasily at the unwonted stillness in his house. Apparently no one was getting ready for church. Could it be that they were not going; that this thing was to be carried to the last ditch? He decided to go and investigate.

His investigations were brief, but entirely conclusive. For the second time that day he was spurned, and by a friend. This time it was the deacon himself who drove him from his wife's room, whither he had betaken him with true instinct to ascertain the household intentions. The deacon seemed to be, if anything, in a worse humor than even Jack himself. The

JACK'S SERMON

doctor had told him that afternoon that Mrs. Pratt was a very sick woman, and that, if she was to pull through at all, she must be kept from all worriment in an atmosphere which fairly bristled with it. The deacon felt that he had a contract on his hands which might prove too heavy for him. He felt, too, with bitterness, that he was an ill-used man, that all his years of faithful labor in the vineyard went for nothing because of some wretched heresy which the enemy had devised to wreck it; and all his humbled pride and his pent-up wrath gathered itself into the kick with which he sent poor Jack flying back where he had come from. It was clear that the deacon was not going to church.

Lonely and forsaken, Jack took his old seat on the porch and pondered. The wrinkles in his brow multiplied and grew deeper as he looked down the road and saw the Joneses, the Smiths, and the Allens go by toward the church. When the Merritts had passed, too, under the lamp, he knew that it must be nearly time for the sermon. They always came in after the long prayer. Jack took a turn up and down the porch, whined at the door once, and, receiving no answer, set off down the road by himself.

The church was filled. It had never looked handsomer. The rival factions had vied with each other in decorating it. Spruce and hemlock sprouted everywhere, and garlands of ground-ivy festooned walls and chancel. The delicious odor of balsam and of burning wax-candles was in the air. The people were all there in their Sunday clothes and the old minister in the pulpit; but the Sunday feeling was not there. Something was not right. Deacon Pratt's pew alone of them all was empty, and the congregation cast wistful glances at it, some secretly behind their hymn-books, others openly and sorrowfully. What the doctor had said in the afternoon had got out. He himself had told Mrs. Mills that it was doubtful if the deacon's wife got around, and it sat heavily upon the conscience of the people.

The opening hymns were sung; the Merritts, late as usual, had taken their seats. The minister took up the Book to read the Christmas gospel from the second chapter of Luke. He had been there longer than most of those who were in the church to-night could remember, had grown old with the people, had loved them as the shepherd who is answerable to the Master for his flock. Their griefs and their troubles were his. If he could not ward them off, he could suffer with them. His voice trembled a little as he read of the tidings of great joy. Perhaps it was age; but it grew firmer as he proceeded toward the end:—

"And suddenly there was with the angel a multitude of the heavenly host praising God and saying, 'Glory to God in the highest, and on earth peace, good-will toward men.'"

The old minister closed the Book and looked out over the congregation. He looked long and yearningly, and twice he cleared his throat, only to repeat, "on earth peace, good-will toward men." The people settled back in their seats, uneasily; they strangely avoided the eye of their pastor. It rested in its slow survey of the flock upon Deacon Pratt's empty pew. And at that moment a strange thing occurred.

Why it should seem strange was, perhaps, not the least strange part of it. Jack had come in alone before. He knew the trick of the door-latch, and had often opened it unaided. He was in the habit of attending the church with the folks; there was no reason why they should not expect him, unless they knew of one themselves. But somehow the click of the latch went clear through the congregation as the heavenly message of good-will had not. All eyes were turned upon the deacon's pew; and they waited.

Jack came slowly and gravely up the aisle and stopped at his master's pew. He sniffed of the empty seat disapprovingly once or twice—he had never seen it in that state before—then he climbed up and sat, serious and attentive as he was wont, in his old seat, facing the pulpit, nodding once as who should say, "I'm here; proceed!"

It is recorded that not even a titter was heard from the Sunday-school, which was out in force. In the silence that reigned in the church was heard only a smothered sob. The old minister looked with misty eyes at his friend. He took off his spectacles, wiped them and put them on again, and tried to speak; but the tears ran down his cheeks and choked his voice. The congregation wept with him.

"Brethren," he said, when he could speak, "glory to God in the highest, and on earth peace, good-will toward men! Jack has preached a better sermon than I can to-night. Let us pray together."

It is further recorded that the first and only quarrel in the Brownville church ended on Christmas Eve and was never heard of again, and that it was all the work of Jack's sermon.

MERRY CHRISTMAS IN THE TENEMENTS

It was just a sprig of holly, with scarlet berries showing against the green, stuck in, by one of the office boys probably, behind the sign that pointed the way up to the editorial rooms. There was no reason why it should have made me start when I came suddenly upon it at the turn of the stairs; but it did. Perhaps it was because that dingy hall, given over to dust and draughts all the days of the year, was the last place in which I expected to meet with any sign of Christmas; perhaps it was because I myself had nearly forgotten the holiday. Whatever the cause, it gave me quite a turn.

I stood, and stared at it. It looked dry, almost withered. Probably it had come a long way. Not much holly grows about Printing-House Square, except in the colored supplements, and that is scarcely of a kind to stir tender memories. Withered and dry, this did. I thought, with a twinge of conscience, of secret little conclaves of my children, of private views of things hidden from mamma at the bottom of drawers, of wild flights when papa appeared unbidden in the door, which I had allowed for once to pass unheeded. Absorbed in the business of the office, I had hardly thought of Christmas coming on, until now it was here. And this sprig of holly on the wall that had come to remind me,—come nobody knew how far,—did it grow yet in the beech-wood clearings, as it did when I gathered it as a boy, tracking through the snow? "Christ-thorn" we called it in our Danish tongue. The red berries, to our simple faith, were the drops of blood that fell from the Saviour's brow as it drooped under its cruel crown upon the cross.

Back to the long ago wandered my thoughts: to the moss-grown beech in which I cut my name and that of a little girl with yellow curls, of blessed memory, with the first jack-knife I ever owned; to the story-book with the little fir tree that pined because it was small, and because the hare jumped over it, and would not be content though the wind and the sun kissed it, and the dews wept over it and told it to rejoice in its young life; and that was so proud when, in the second year, the hare had to go round it, because then it knew it was getting big,—Hans Christian Andersen's story that we loved above all the rest; for we knew the tree right well, and the hare; even the tracks it left in the snow we had seen. Ah, those were the Yule-tide seasons, when the old Domkirke shone with a thousand wax candles on Christmas eve; when all business was laid aside to let the world make merry one whole week; when big red apples were roasted on the stove, and bigger doughnuts were baked within it for the long feast! Never such had been known since. Christmas to-day is but a name, a memory.

A door slammed below, and let in the noises of the street. The holly rustled in the draught. Some one going out said, "A Merry Christmas to you all!" in a big, hearty voice. I awoke from my revery to find myself back in New York with a glad glow at the heart. It was not true. I had only forgotten. It was myself that had changed, not Christmas. That was here, with the old cheer, the old message of good-will, the old royal road to the heart of mankind. How often had I seen its blessed charity, that never corrupts, make light in the hovels of darkness and despair! how often watched its spirit of self-sacrifice and devotion in those who had, besides themselves, nothing to give! and as often the sight had made whole my faith in human nature. No! Christmas was not of the past, its spirit not dead. The lad who fixed the sprig of holly on the stairs knew it; my reporter's note-book bore witness to it. Witness of my contrition for the wrong I did the gentle spirit of the holiday, here let the book tell the story of one Christmas in the tenements of the poor:—

It is evening in Grand Street. The shops east and west are pouring forth their swarms of workers. Street and sidewalk are filled with an eager throng of young men and women, chatting gayly, and elbowing the jam of holiday shoppers that linger about the big stores. The street-cars labor along, loaded down to the steps with passengers carrying bundles of every size and odd shape. Along the curb a string of pedlers hawk penny

MERRY CHRISTMAS IN THE TENEMENTS

toys in push-carts with noisy clamor, fearless for once of being moved on by the police. Christmas brings a two weeks' respite from persecution even to the friendless street-fakir. From the window of one brilliantly lighted store a bevy of mature dolls in dishabille stretch forth their arms appealingly to a troop of factory-hands passing by. The young men chaff the girls, who shriek with laughter and run. The policeman on the corner stops beating his hands together to keep warm, and makes a mock attempt to catch them, whereat their shrieks rise shriller than ever. "Them stockin's o' yourn 'll be the death o' Santa Claus!" he shouts after them, as they dodge. And they, looking back, snap saucily, "Mind yer business, freshy!" But their laughter belies their words. "They giv' it to ye straight that time," grins the grocer's clerk, come out to snatch a look at the crowds; and the two swap holiday greetings.

At the corner, where two opposing tides of travel form an eddy, the line of push-carts debouches down the darker side street. In its gloom their torches burn with a fitful glare that wakes black shadows among the trusses of the railroad structure overhead. A woman, with worn shawl drawn tightly about head and shoulders, bargains with a pedler for a monkey on a stick and two cents' worth of flitter-gold. Five ill-clad youngsters flatten their noses against the frozen pane of the toy-shop, in ecstasy at something there, which proves to be a milk wagon, with driver, horses, and cans that can be unloaded. It is something their minds can grasp. One comes forth with a penny goldfish of pasteboard clutched tightly in his hand, and, casting cautious glances right and left, speeds across the way to the door of a tenement, where a little girl stands waiting. "It's yer Chris'mas, Kate," he says, and thrusts it into her eager fist. The black doorway swallows them up.

Across the narrow yard, in the basement of the rear house, the lights of a Christmas tree show against the grimy window pane. The hare would never have gone around it, it is so very small. The two children are busily engaged fixing the goldfish upon one of its branches. Three little candles that burn there shed light upon a scene of utmost desolation. The room is black with smoke and dirt. In the middle of the floor oozes an oil-stove that serves at once to take the raw edge off the cold and to cook the meals by. Half the window panes are broken, and the holes stuffed with rags. The sleeve of an old coat hangs out of one, and beats drearily upon the sash when the wind sweeps over the fence and rattles the rotten shutters. The family wash, clammy and gray, hangs on a clothes-line stretched across the room. Under it, at a table set with cracked and empty plates, a discouraged woman sits eying the children's show gloomily. It is evident that she has been drinking. The peaked faces of the little ones wear a famished look. There are three—the third an infant, put to bed in what was once a baby carriage. The two from the street are pulling it around to get the tree in range. The baby sees it, and crows with delight. The boy shakes a branch, and the goldfish leaps and sparkles in the candle-light.

"See, sister!" he pipes; "see Santa Claus!" And they clap their hands in glee. The woman at the table wakes out of her stupor, gazes around her, and bursts into a fit of maudlin weeping.

The door falls to. Five flights up, another opens upon a bare attic room which a patient little woman is setting to rights. There are only three chairs, a box, and a bedstead in the room, but they take a deal of careful arranging. The bed hides the broken plaster in the wall through which the wind came in; each chair-leg stands over a rat-hole, at once to hide it and to keep the rats out. One is left; the box is for that. The plaster of the ceiling is held up with pasteboard patches. I know the story of that attic. It is one of cruel desertion. The woman's husband is even now living in plenty with the creature for whom he forsook her, not a dozen blocks away, while she "keeps the home together for the childer." She sought justice, but the lawyer demanded a retainer; so she gave it up, and went back to her little ones. For this room that barely keeps the winter wind out she pays four dollars a month, and is behind with the rent. There is scarce bread in the house; but the spirit of Christmas has found her attic. Against a broken wall is tacked a hemlock branch, the leavings of the corner grocer's fitting-block; pink string from the packing-counter hangs on it in festoons. A tallow dip on the box furnishes the illumination. The children sit up in bed, and watch it with shining eyes.

"We're having Christmas!" they say.

The lights of the Bowery glow like a myriad twinkling stars upon the ceaseless flood of humanity that surges ever through the great highway of the homeless. They shine upon long rows of lodging-houses, in which hundreds of young men, cast helpless upon the reef of the strange city, are learning their first lessons of utter loneliness; for what desolation is there like that of the careless crowd when all the world rejoices? They shine upon the tempter setting his snares there, and upon the missionary and the Salvation Army lass, disputing his catch with him; upon the police detective going his rounds with coldly observant eye intent upon the outcome of the contest; upon the wreck that is past hope, and upon the youth pausing on the verge of the pit in which the other has long ceased

MERRY CHRISTMAS IN THE TENEMENTS

to struggle. Sights and sounds of Christmas there are in plenty in the Bowery. Balsam and hemlock and fir stand in groves along the busy thoroughfare, and garlands of green embower mission and dive impartially. Once a year the old street recalls its youth with an effort. It is true that it is largely a commercial effort; that the evergreen, with an instinct that is not of its native hills, haunts saloon-corners by preference; but the smell of the pine woods is in the air, and—Christmas is not too critical—one is grateful for the effort. It varies with the opportunity. At "Beefsteak John's" it is content with artistically embalming crullers and mince-pies in green cabbage under the window lamp. Over yonder, where the mile-post of the old lane still stands,—in its unhonored old age become the vehicle of publishing the latest "sure cure" to the world,—a florist, whose undenominational zeal for the holiday and trade outstrips alike distinction of creed and property, has transformed the sidewalk and the ugly railroad structure into a veritable bower, spanning it with a canopy of green, under which dwell with him, in neighborly good-will, the Young Men's Christian Association and the Jewish tailor next door.

In the next block a "turkey-shoot" is in progress. Crowds are trying their luck at breaking the glass balls that dance upon tiny jets of water in front of a marine view with the moon rising, yellow and big, out of a silver sea. A man-of-war, with lights burning aloft, labors under a rocky coast. Groggy sailormen, on shore leave, make unsteady attempts upon the dancing balls. One mistakes the moon for the target, but is discovered in season. "Don't shoot that," says the man who loads the guns; "there's a lamp behind it." Three scared birds in the window recess try vainly to snatch a moment's sleep between shots and the trains that go roaring overhead on the elevated road. Roused by the sharp crack of the rifles, they blink at the lights in the street, and peck moodily at a crust in their bed of shavings.

The dime museum gong clatters out its noisy warning that "the lecture" is about to begin. From the concert hall, where men sit drinking beer in clouds of smoke, comes the thin voice of a short-skirted singer, warbling, "Do they think of me at home?" The young fellow who sits near the door, abstractedly making figures in the wet track of the "schooners," buries something there with a sudden restless turn, and calls for another beer. Out in the street a band strikes up. A host with banners advances, chanting an unfamiliar hymn. In the ranks marches a cripple on crutches. Newsboys follow, gaping. Under the illuminated clock of the Cooper Institute the procession halts, and the leader, turning his face to the sky, offers a prayer. The passing crowds stop to listen. A few bare their heads. The devoted group, the flapping banners, and the changing torch-light on upturned faces, make a strange, weird picture. Then the drum-beat, and the band files into its barracks across the street. A few of the listeners follow, among them the lad from the concert hall, who slinks shamefacedly in when he thinks no one is looking.

Down at the foot of the Bowery is the "panhandlers' beat," where the saloons elbow one another at every step, crowding out all other business than that of keeping lodgers to support them. Within call of it, across the square, stands a church which, in the memory of men yet living, was built to shelter the fashionable Baptist audiences of a day when Madison Square was out in the fields, and Harlem had a foreign sound. The fashionable audiences are gone long since. To-day the church, fallen into premature decay, but still handsome in its strong and noble lines, stands as a missionary outpost in the land of the enemy, its builders would have said, doing a greater work than they planned. To-night is the Christmas festival of its English-speaking Sunday-school, and the pews are filled. The banners of United Italy, of modern Hellas, of France and Germany and England, hang side by side with the Chinese dragon and the starry flag—signs of the cosmopolitan character of the congregation. Greek and Roman Catholics, Jews and joss-worshippers, go there; few Protestants, and no Baptists. It is easy to pick out the children in their seats by nationality, and as easy to read the story of poverty and suffering that stands written in more than one mother's haggard face, now beaming with pleasure at the little ones' glee. A gayly decorated Christmas tree has taken the place of the pulpit. At its foot is stacked a mountain of bundles, Santa Claus's gifts to the school. A self-conscious young man with soap-locks has just been allowed to retire, amid tumultuous applause, after blowing "Nearer, My God, to Thee" on his horn until his cheeks swelled almost to bursting. A trumpet ever takes the Fourth Ward by storm. A class of little girls is climbing upon the platform. Each wears a capital letter on her breast, and has a piece to speak that begins with the letter; together they spell its lesson. There is momentary consternation; one is missing. As the discovery is made, a child pushes past the door-keeper, hot and breathless. "I am in 'Boundless Love,'" she says, and makes for the platform, where her arrival restores confidence and the language.

In the audience the befrocked visitor from up-town sits cheek by jowl with the pigtailed Chinaman and the dark-browed Italian. Up in the gallery, farthest from the preacher's desk and the tree, sits a Jewish mother with three boys, almost in rags. A dingy and threadbare shawl partly hides her poor calico wrap and patched apron. The woman shrinks in the pew, fearful of being seen; her boys stand upon the benches, and applaud with the rest. She endeavors vainly to restrain them. "Tick, tick!" goes the old clock over the door through which wealth and fashion went out long years ago, and poverty came in.

Tick, tick! the world moves, with us—without; without or with. She is the yesterday, they the to-morrow. What shall the harvest be?

Loudly ticked the old clock in time with the doxology, the other day, when they cleared the tenants out of Gotham Court down here in Cherry Street, and shut the iron doors of Single and Double Alley against them. Never did the world move faster or surer toward a better day than when the wretched slum was seized by the health officers as a nuisance unfit longer to disgrace a Christian city. The snow lies deep in the deserted passsageways, and the vacant floors are given over to evil smells, and to the rats that forage in squads, burrowing in the neglected sewers. The "wall of wrath" still towers above the buildings in the adjoining Alderman's Court, but its wrath at last is wasted.

It was built by a vengeful Quaker, whom the alderman had knocked down in a quarrel over the boundary line, and transmitted its legacy of hate to generations yet unborn; for where it stood it shut out sunlight and air from the tenements of Alderman's Court. And at last it is to go, Gotham Court and all; and to the going the wall of wrath has contributed its share, thus in the end atoning for some of the harm it wrought. Tick! old clock; the world moves. Never yet did Christmas seem less dark on Cherry Hill than since the lights were put out in Gotham Court forever.

In "The Bend" the philanthropist undertaker who "buries for what he can catch on the plate" hails the Yule-tide season with a pyramid of green made of two coffins set on end. It has been a good day, he says cheerfully, putting up the shutters; and his mind is easy. But the "good days" of The Bend are over, too. The Bend itself is all but gone. Where the old pig-sty stood, children dance and sing to the strumming of a cracked piano-organ propelled on wheels by an Italian and his wife. The park that has come to take the place of the slum will curtail the undertaker's profits, as it has lessened the work of the police. Murder was the fashion of the day that is past. Scarce a knife has been drawn since the sunlight shone into that evil spot, and grass and green shrubs took the place of the old rookeries. The Christmas gospel of peace and good-will moves in where the slum moves out. It never had a chance before.

The children follow the organ, stepping in the slush to the music, bareheaded and with torn shoes, but happy; across the Five Points and through "the Bay,"—known to the directory as Baxter Street,—to "the Divide," still Chatham Street to its denizens, though the aldermen have rechristened it Park Row. There other delegations of Greek and Italian children meet and escort the music on its homeward trip. In one of the crooked streets near the river its journey comes to an end. A battered door opens to let it in. A tallow dip burns sleepily on the creaking stairs. The water runs with a loud clatter in the sink: it is to keep it from freezing. There is not a whole window pane in the hall. Time was when this was a fine house harboring wealth and refinement. It has neither now. In the old parlor downstairs a knot of hard-faced men and women sit on benches about a deal table, playing cards. They have a jug between them, from which they drink by turns. On the stump of a mantel-shelf a lamp burns before a rude print of the Mother of God. No one pays any heed to the hand-organ man and his wife as they climb to their attic. There is a colony of them up there—three families in four rooms.

"Come in, Antonio," says the tenant of the double flat,—the one with two rooms,—"come and keep Christmas." Antonio enters, cap in hand. In the corner by the dormer-window a "crib" has been fitted up in commemoration of the Nativity. A soap-box and two hemlock branches are the elements. Six tallow candles and a night-light illuminate a singular collection of rarities, set out with much ceremonial show. A doll tightly wrapped in swaddling-clothes represents "the Child." Over it stands a ferocious-looking beast, easily recognized as a survival of the last political campaign,—the Tammany tiger,—threatening to swallow it at a gulp if one as much as takes one's eyes off it. A miniature Santa Claus, a pasteboard monkey, and several other articles of bric-à-brac of the kind the tenement affords, complete the outfit. The background is a picture of St. Donato, their village saint, with the Madonna "whom they worship most." But the incongruity harbors no suggestion of disrespect. The children view the strange show with genuine reverence, bowing and crossing themselves before it. There are five, the oldest a girl of seventeen, who works for a sweater, making three dollars a week. It is all the money that comes in, for the father has been sick and unable to work eight months and the mother has her hands full: the youngest is a baby in arms. Three of the children go to a charity school, where they are fed, a great help, now the holidays have come to make work slack for sister. The rent is six dollars—two weeks' pay out of the four. The mention of a possible chance of light work for the man brings the daughter with her sewing from the adjoining room, eager to hear. That would be Christmas indeed! "Pietro!" She runs to the neighbors to communicate the joyful tidings. Pietro comes, with his new-born baby, which he is tending while his wife lies ill, to look at the maestro, so powerful and good. He also has been out of work for months, with a family of mouths to fill, and nothing coming in. His children are all small yet, but they speak English.

"What," I say, holding a silver dime up before the oldest, a smart little chap of seven—"what would you do if I gave you this?"

"Get change," he replies promptly. When he is told that it is his own, to buy toys with, his eyes open wide with wondering incredulity. By degrees he understands. The father does not. He looks questioningly from one to the other. When told, his respect increases visibly for "the rich gentleman."

They were villagers of the same community in southern Italy, these people and others in the tenements thereabouts, and they moved their patron saint with them. They cluster about his worship here, but the worship is more than an empty form. He typifies to them the old neighborliness of home, the spirit of mutual help, of charity, and of the common cause against the common enemy. The community life survives through their saint in the far city to an unsuspected extent. The sick are cared for; the dreaded hospital is fenced out. There are no Italian evictions. The saint has paid the rent of this attic through two hard months; and here at his shrine the Calabrian village gathers, in the persons of these three, to do him honor on Christmas Eve.

Where the old Africa has been made over into a modern Italy, since King Humbert's cohorts struck the up-town trail, three hundred of the little foreigners are having an uproarious time over their Christmas tree in the Children's Aid Society's school. And well they may, for the like has not been seen in Sullivan Street in this generation. Christmas trees are rather rarer over here than on the East Side, where the German leavens the lump with his loyalty to home traditions. This is loaded with silver and gold and toys without end, until there is little left of the original green. Santa Claus's sleigh must have been upset in a snow-drift over here, and righted by throwing the cargo overboard, for there is at least a wagon-load of things that can find no room on the tree. The appearance of "teacher" with a double armful of curly-headed dolls in red, yellow, and green Mother-Hubbards, doubtful how to dispose of them, provokes a shout of approval, which is presently quieted by the principal's bell.

School is "in" for the preliminary exercises. Afterward there are to be the tree and ice-cream for the good children. In their anxiety to prove their title clear, they sit so straight, with arms folded, that the whole row bends over backward. The lesson is brief, the answers to the point.

"What do we receive at Christmas?" the teacher wants to know. The whole school responds with a shout, "Dolls and toys!" To the question, "Why do we receive them at Christmas?" the answer is not so prompt. But one youngster from Thompson Street holds up his hand. He knows. "Because we always get 'em," he says; and the class is convinced: it is a fact. A baby wails because it cannot get the whole tree at once. The "little mother"—herself a child of less than a dozen winters—who has it in charge, cooes over it, and soothes its grief with the aid of a surreptitious sponge-cake evolved from the depths of teacher's pocket. Babies are encouraged in these schools, though not originally included in their plan, as often the one condition upon which the older children can be reached. Some one has to mind the baby, with all hands out at work.

The school sings "Santa Lucia" and "Children of the Heavenly King," and baby is lulled to sleep.

"Who is this King?" asks the teacher, suddenly, at the end of a verse. Momentary stupefaction. The little minds are on ice-cream just then; the lad nearest the door has telegraphed that it is being carried up in pails. A little fellow on the back seat saves the day. Up goes his brown fist.

"Well, Vito, who is he?"

"McKinley!" pipes the lad, who remembers the election just past; and the school adjourns for ice-cream.

It is a sight to see them eat it. In a score of such schools, from the Hook to Harlem, the sight is enjoyed in Christmas week by the men and women who, out of their own pockets, reimburse Santa Claus for his outlay, and count it a joy, as well they may; for their beneficence sometimes makes the one bright spot in lives that have suffered of all wrongs the most cruel,—that of being despoiled of their childhood. Sometimes they are little Bohemians; sometimes the children of refugee Jews; and again, Italians, or the descendants of the Irish stock of Hell's Kitchen and Poverty Row; always the poorest, the shabbiest, the hungriest—the children Santa Claus loves best to find, if any one will show him the way. Having so much on hand, he has no time, you see, to look them up himself. That must be done for him; and it is done. To the teacher in the Sullivan Street school came one little girl, this last Christmas, with anxious inquiry if it was true that he came around with toys.

"I hanged my stocking last time," she said, "and he didn't come at all." In the front house indeed, he left a drum and a doll, but no message from him reached the rear house in the alley. "Maybe he couldn't find it," she said soberly. Did the teacher think he would come if she wrote to him? She had learned to write.

Together they composed a note to Santa Claus, speaking for a doll and a bell—the bell to play "go to school" with when she was kept home minding the baby. Lest he should by any chance miss the alley in spite of directions, little Rosa was invited to hang her stocking, and her sister's, with the janitor's children's in the school. And lo! on Christmas morning there was a gorgeous doll, and a bell that was a whole curriculum in itself, as good as a year's schooling any day! Faith in Santa Claus is established in that Thompson Street alley for this generation at least; and Santa Claus, got by hook or by crook into an Eighth Ward alley, is as good as the whole Supreme Court bench, with the Court of Appeals thrown in, for backing the Board of Health against the slum.

But the ice-cream! They eat it off the seats, half of them kneeling or squatting on the floor; they blow on it, and put it in their pockets to carry home to baby. Two little shavers discovered to be feeding each other, each watching the smack develop on the other's lips as the acme of his own bliss, are "cousins"; that is why. Of cake there is a double supply. It is a dozen years since "Fighting Mary," the wildest child in the Seventh Avenue school, taught them a lesson there which they have never forgotten. She was perfectly untamable, fighting everybody in school, the despair of her teacher, till on Thanksgiving, reluctantly included in the general amnesty and mince-pie, she was caught cramming the pie into her pocket, after eyeing it with a look of pure ecstasy, but refusing to touch it. "For mother" was her explanation, delivered with a defiant look before which the class quailed. It is recorded, but not in the minutes, that the board of managers wept over Fighting Mary, who, all unconscious of having caused such an astonishing "break," was at that moment engaged in maintaining her prestige and reputation by fighting the gang in the next block. The minutes contain merely a formal resolution to the effect that occasions of mince-pie shall carry double rations thenceforth. And the rule has been kept—not only in Seventh Avenue, but in every industrial school—since. Fighting Mary won the biggest fight of her troubled life that day, without striking a blow.

It was in the Seventh Avenue school last Christmas that I offered the truant class a four-bladed penknife as a prize for whittling out the truest

Maltese cross. It was a class of black sheep, and it was the blackest sheep of the flock that won the prize. "That awful Savarese," said the principal in despair. I thought of Fighting Mary, and bade her take heart. I regret to say that within a week the hapless Savarese was black-listed for banking up the school door with snow, so that not even the janitor could get out and at him.

Within hail of the Sullivan Street school camps a scattered little band, the Christmas customs of which I had been trying for years to surprise. They are Indians, a handful of Mohawks and Iroquois, whom some ill wind has blown down from their Canadian reservation, and left in these West Side tenements to eke out such a living as they can, weaving mats and baskets, and threading glass pearls on slippers and pin-cushions, until, one after another, they have died off and gone to happier hunting-grounds than Thompson Street. There were as many families as one could count on the fingers of both hands when I first came upon them, at the death of old Tamenund, the basket maker. Last Christmas there were seven. I had about made up my mind that the only real Americans in New York did not keep the holiday at all, when, one Christmas Eve, they showed me how. Just as dark was setting in, old Mrs. Benoit came from her Hudson Street attic—where she was known among the neighbors, as old and poor as she, as Mrs. Ben Wah, and was believed to be the relict of a warrior of the name of Benjamin Wah—to the office of the Charity Organization Society, with a bundle for a friend who had helped her over a rough spot—the rent, I suppose. The bundle was done up elaborately in blue cheese-cloth, and contained a lot of little garments which she had made out of the remnants of blankets and cloth of her own from a younger and better day. "For those," she said, in her French patois, "who are poorer than myself;" and hobbled away. I found out, a few days later, when I took her picture weaving mats in her attic room, that she had scarcely food in the house that Christmas Day and not the car fare to take her to church! Walking was bad, and her old limbs were stiff. She sat by the window through the winter evening, and watched the sun go down behind the western hills, comforted by her pipe. Mrs. Ben Wah, to give her her local name, is not really an Indian; but her husband was one, and she lived all her life with the tribe till she came here. She is a philosopher in her own quaint way. "It is no disgrace to be poor," said she to me, regarding her empty tobacco-pouch; "but it is sometimes a great inconvenience." Not even the recollection of the vote of censure that was passed upon me once by the ladies of the Charitable Ten for surreptitiously supplying an aged couple, the special object of their charity, with army plug, could have deterred me from taking the hint.

Very likely, my old friend Miss Sherman, in her Broome Street cellar, —it is always the attic or the cellar,—would object to Mrs. Ben Wah's claim to being the only real American in my note-book. She is from Down East, and says "stun" for stone. In her youth she was lady's-maid to a general's wife, the recollection of which military career equally condones the cellar and prevents her holding any sort of communication with her common neighbors, who add to the offence of being foreigners the unpardonable one of being mostly men. Eight cats bear her steady company, and keep alive her starved affections. I found them on last Christmas Eve behind barricaded doors; for the cold that had locked the water-pipes had brought the neighbors down to the cellar, where Miss Sherman's cunning had kept them from freezing. Their tin pans and buckets were even then banging against her door. "They're a miserable lot," said the old maid, fondling her cats defiantly; "but let 'em. It's Christmas. Ah!" she added, as one of the eight stood up in her lap and rubbed its cheek against hers, "they're innocent. It isn't poor little animals that does the harm. It's men and women that does it to each other." I don't know whether it was just philosophy, like Mrs. Ben Wah's, or a glimpse of her story. If she had one, she kept it for her cats.

In a hundred places all over the city, when Christmas comes, as many open-air fairs spring suddenly into life. A kind of Gentile Feast of Tabernacles possesses the tenement districts especially. Green-embowered booths stand in rows at the curb, and the voice of the tin trumpet is heard in the land. The common source of all the show is down by the North River, in the district known as "the Farm." Down there Santa Claus establishes headquarters early in December and until past New Year. The broad quay looks then more like a clearing in a pine forest than a busy section of the metropolis. The steamers discharge their loads of fir trees at the piers until they stand stacked mountain-high, with foot-hills of holly and ground-ivy trailing off toward the land side. An army train of wagons is engaged in carting them away from early morning till late at night; but the green forest grows, in spite of it all, until in places it shuts the shipping out of sight altogether. The air is redolent with the smell of balsam and pine. After nightfall, when the lights are burning in the busy market, and the homeward-bound crowds with baskets and heavy burdens of Christmas greens jostle one another with good-natured banter,—nobody is ever cross down here in the holiday season,—it is good to take a stroll through the Farm, if one has a spot in his heart faithful yet to the hills and the woods in spite of the latter-day city. But it is when the moonlight is upon the water and upon the dark phantom forest, when the heavy breathing of some passing steamer is the only sound that breaks the stillness of the night, and the watchman smokes his only pipe on the bulwark, that the Farm has a mood and an atmosphere all its own, full of poetry which some day a painter's brush will catch and hold.

Into the ugliest tenement street Christmas brings something of picturesqueness, of cheer. Its message was ever to the poor and the heavy-laden, and by them it is understood with an instinctive yearning to do it honor. In the stiff dignity of the brown-stone streets up-town there may be scarce a hint of it. In the homes of the poor it blossoms on stoop and fire-escape, looks out of the front window, and makes the unsightly barber-pole to sprout overnight like an Aaron's-rod. Poor indeed is the home that has not its sign of peace over the hearth, be it but a single sprig of green. A little color creeps with it even into rabbinical Hester Street, and shows in the shop-windows and in the children's faces. The very feather dusters in the pedler's stock take on brighter hues for the occasion, and the big knives in the cutler's shop gleam with a lively anticipation of the impending goose "with fixin's"—a concession, perhaps, to the commercial rather than the religious holiday: business comes then, if ever. A crowd of ragamuffins camp out at a window where Santa Claus and his wife stand in state, embodiment of the domestic ideal that has not yet gone out of fashion in these tenements, gazing hungrily at the announcement that "A silver present will be given to every purchaser by a real Santa Claus.—M. Levitsky." Across the way, in a hole in the wall, two cobblers are pegging away under an oozy lamp that makes a yellow splurge on the inky blackness about them, revealing to the passer-by their bearded faces, but nothing of the environment save a single sprig of holly suspended from the lamp. From what forgotten brake it came with a message of cheer, a thought of wife and children across the sea waiting their summons, God knows. The shop is their house and home. It was once the hall of the tenement; but to save space, enough has been walled in to make room for their bench and bed; the tenants go through the next house. No matter if they are cramped; by and by they will have room. By and by comes the spring, and with it the steamer. Does not the green branch speak of spring and of hope? The policeman on the beat hears their hammers beat a joyous tattoo past midnight, far into Christmas morning. Who shall say its message has not reached even them in their slum?

Where the noisy trains speed over the iron highway past the second-story windows of Allen Street, a cellar door yawns darkly in the shadow of one of the pillars that half block the narrow sidewalk. A dull gleam behind the cobweb-shrouded window pane supplements the sign over the door, in Yiddish and English: "Old Brasses." Four crooked and mouldy steps lead to utter darkness, with no friendly voice to guide the hapless customer. Fumbling along the dank wall, he is left to find the door of the shop as best he can. Not a likely place to encounter the fastidious from the Avenue! Yet ladies in furs and silk find this door and the grim old smith within it. Now and then an artist stumbles upon them, and exults exceedingly in his find. Two holiday shoppers are even now haggling with the coppersmith over the price of a pair of curiously wrought brass candlesticks. The old man has turned from the forge, at which he was working, unmindful of his callers roving among the dusty shelves. Standing there, erect and sturdy, in his shiny leather apron, hammer in hand, with the firelight upon his venerable head, strong arms bared to the elbow, and the square paper cap pushed back from a thoughtful, knotty brow, he stirs strange fancies. One half expects to see him fashioning a gorget or a sword on his anvil. But his is a more peaceful craft. Nothing more warlike is in sight than a row of brass shields, destined for ornament, not for battle. Dark shadows chase one another by the flickering light among copper kettles of ruddy glow, old-fashioned samovars, and massive andirons of tarnished brass. The bargaining goes on. Overhead the nineteenth century speeds by with rattle and roar; in here linger the shadows of the centuries long dead. The boy at the anvil listens open-mouthed, clutching the bellows-rope.

In Liberty Hall a Jewish wedding is in progress. Liberty! Strange how the word echoes through these sweaters' tenements, where starvation is at home half the time. It is an all-consuming passion with these people, whose spirit a thousand years of bondage have not availed to daunt. It breaks out in strikes, when to strike is to hunger and die. Not until I stood by a striking cloak-maker whose last cent was gone, with not a crust in the house to feed seven hungry mouths, yet who had voted vehemently in the meeting that day to keep up the strike to the bitter end,—bitter indeed, nor far distant,—and heard him at sunset recite the prayer of his fathers: "Blessed art thou, O Lord our God, King of the world, that thou hast redeemed us as thou didst redeem our fathers, hast delivered us from bondage to liberty, and from servile dependence to redemption!"—not until then did I know what of sacrifice the word might mean, and how utterly we of another day had forgotten. But for once shop and tenement are left behind. Whatever other days may have in store, this is their day of play, when all may rejoice.

The bridegroom, a cloak-presser in a hired dress suit, sits alone and ill at ease at one end of the hall, sipping whiskey with a fine air of indifference, but glancing apprehensively toward the crowd of women in the opposite corner that surround the bride, a pale little shop-girl with a pleading, winsome face. From somewhere unexpectedly appears a big man in an ill-fitting coat and skullcap, flanked on either side by a fiddler, who scrapes away and away, accompanying the improvisator in a plaintive minor key as he halts before the bride and intones his lay. With many a shrug of stooping shoulders and queer excited gesture, he drones, in the harsh, guttural Yiddish of Hester Street, his story of life's joys and sorrows, its struggles and victories in the land of promise. The women listen, nodding and swaying their bodies sympathetically. He works himself into a frenzy, in which the fiddlers vainly try to keep up with him. He turns and digs the laggard angrily in the side without losing the metre. The climax comes. The bride bursts into hysterical sobs, while the women wipe their eyes. A plate, heretofore concealed under his coat, is whisked out. He has conquered; the inevitable collection is taken up.

The tuneful procession moves upon the bridegroom. An Essex Street girl in the crowd, watching them go, says disdainfully: "None of this humbug when I get married." It is the straining of young America at the fetters of tradition. Ten minutes later, when, between double files of women holding candles, the couple pass to the canopy where the rabbi waits, she has already forgotten; and when the crunching of a glass under the bridegroom's heel announces that they are one, and that until the broken pieces be reunited he is hers and hers alone, she joins with all the company in the exulting shout of "Mozzel tov!" ("Good luck!"). Then the *dupka*, men and women joining in, forgetting all but the moment, hands on hips, stepping in time, forward, backward, and across. And then the feast.

They sit at the long tables by squads and tribes. Those who belong together sit together. There is no attempt at pairing off for conversation or mutual entertainment, at speech-making or toasting. The business in hand is to eat, and it is attended to. The bridegroom, at the head of the table, with his shiny silk hat on, sets the example; and the guests emulate it with zeal, the men smoking big, strong cigars between mouthfuls. "Gosh! ain't it fine?" is the grateful comment of one curly-headed youngster, bravely attacking his third plate of chicken-stew. "Fine as silk," nods his neighbor in knickerbockers. Christmas, for once, means something to them that they can understand. The crowd of hurrying waiters make room for one bearing aloft a small turkey adorned with much tinsel and many paper flowers. It is for the bride, the one thing not to be touched until the next day—one day off from the drudgery of housekeeping; she, too, can keep Christmas.

A group of bearded, dark-browed men sit apart, the rabbi among them. They are the orthodox, who cannot break bread with the rest, for fear, though the food be kosher, the plates have been defiled. They brought their own to the feast, and sit at their own table, stern and justified. Did they but know what depravity is harbored in the impish mind of the girl yonder, who plans to hang her stocking overnight by the window! There is no fireplace in the tenement. Queer things happen over here, in the strife between the old and the new. The girls of the College Settlement, last summer, felt compelled to explain that the holiday in the country which they offered some of these children was to be spent in an Episcopal clergyman's house, where they had prayers every morning. "Oh," was the mother's indulgent answer, "they know it isn't true, so it won't hurt them."

The bell of a neighboring church tower strikes the vesper hour. A man in working-clothes uncovers his head reverently, and passes on. Through the vista of green bowers formed of the grocer's stock of Christmas trees a passing glimpse of flaring torches in the distant square is caught. They touch with flame the gilt cross towering high above the "White Garden," as the German residents call Tompkins Square. On the sidewalk the holy-eve fair is in its busiest hour. In the pine-board booths stand rows of staring toy dogs alternately with plaster saints. Red apples and candy are hawked from carts. Pedlers offer colored candles with shrill outcry. A huckster feeding his horse by the curb scatters, unseen, a share for the sparrows. The cross flashes white against the dark sky.

In one of the side streets near the East River has stood for thirty years a little mission church, called Hope Chapel by its founders, in the brave spirit in which they built it. It has had plenty of use for the spirit since. Of the kind of problems that beset its pastor I caught a glimpse the other day, when, as I entered his room, a rough-looking man went out.

"One of my cares," said Mr. Devins, looking after him with contracted brow. "He has spent two Christmas days of twenty-three out of jail. He is a burglar, or was. His daughter has brought him round. She is a seamstress. For three months, now, she has been keeping him and the home, working nights. If I could only get him a job! He won't stay honest long without it; but who wants a burglar for a watchman? And how can I recommend him?"

A few doors from the chapel an alley sets into the block. We halted at the mouth of it.

"Come in," said Mr. Devins, "and wish Blind Jennie a Merry Christmas."

We went in, in single file; there was not room for two. As we climbed the creaking stairs of the rear tenement, a chorus of children's shrill voices burst into song somewhere above.

"It is her class," said the pastor of Hope Chapel, as he stopped on the landing. "They are all kinds. We never could hope to reach them; Jennie can. They fetch her the papers given out in the Sunday-school, and read to her what is printed under the pictures; and she tells them the story of it. There is nothing Jennie doesn't know about the Bible."

The door opened upon a low-ceiled room, where the evening shades lay deep. The red glow from the kitchen stove discovered a jam of children, young girls mostly, perched on the table, the chairs, in one another's laps, or squatting on the floor; in the midst of them, a little old woman with heavily veiled face, and wan, wrinkled hands folded in her lap. The singing ceased as we stepped across the threshold.

"Be welcome," piped a harsh voice with a singular note of cheerfulness in it. "Whose step is that with you, pastor? I don't know it. He is welcome in Jennie's house, whoever he be. Girls, make him to home." The girls moved up to make room.

"Jennie has not seen since she was a child," said the clergyman, gently; "but she knows a friend without it. Some day she shall see the great Friend in his glory, and then she shall be Blind Jennie no more."

The little woman raised the veil from a face shockingly disfigured, and touched the eyeless sockets. "Some day," she repeated, "Jennie shall see. Not long now—not long!" Her pastor patted her hand. The silence of the dark room was broken by Blind Jennie's voice, rising cracked and quavering: "Alas! and did my Saviour bleed?" The shrill chorus burst in:—

> *It was there by faith I received my sight,*
> *And now I am happy all the day.*

MERRY CHRISTMAS IN THE TENEMENTS

The light that falls from the windows of the Neighborhood Guild, in Delancey Street, makes a white path across the asphalt pavement. Within, there is mirth and laughter. The Tenth Ward Social Reform Club is having its Christmas festival. Its members, poor mothers, scrub-women, —the president is the janitress of a tenement near by,—have brought their little ones, a few their husbands, to share in the fun. One little girl has to be dragged up to the grab-bag. She cries at the sight of Santa Claus. The baby has drawn a woolly horse. He kisses the toy with a look of ecstatic bliss, and toddles away. At the far end of the hall a game of blindman's-buff is starting up. The aged grandmother, who has watched it with growing excitement, bids one of the settlement workers hold her grand-child, that she may join in; and she does join in, with all the pent-up hunger of fifty joyless years. The worker, looking on, smiles; one has been reached. Thus is the battle against the slum waged and won with the child's play.

Tramp! tramp! comes the to-morrow upon the stage. Two hundred and fifty pairs of little feet, keeping step, are marching to dinner in the Newsboys' Lodging-house. Five hundred pairs more are restlessly awaiting their turn upstairs. In prison, hospital, and almshouse to-night the city is host, and gives of her plenty. Here an unknown friend has spread a generous repast for the waifs who all the rest of the days shift for themselves as best they can. Turkey, coffee, and pie, with "vegetubles" to fill in. As the file of eagle-eyed youngsters passes down the long tables, there are swift movements of grimy hands, and shirt-waists bulge, ragged coats sag at the pockets. Hardly is the file seated when the plaint rises: "I ain't got no pie! It got swiped on me." Seven despoiled ones hold up their hands.

The superintendent laughs—it is Christmas Eve. He taps one tentatively on the bulging shirt. "What have you here, my lad?"

"Me pie," responds he, with an innocent look; "I wuz scart it would get stole."

A little fellow who has been eying one of the visitors attentively takes his knife out of his mouth, and points it at him with conviction.

"I know you," he pipes. "You're a p'lice commissioner. I seen yer picter in the papers. You're Teddy Roosevelt!"

The clatter of knives and forks ceases suddenly. Seven pies creep stealthily over the edge of the table, and are replaced on as many plates. The visitors laugh. It was a case of mistaken identity.

Farthest down town, where the island narrows toward the Battery, and warehouses crowd the few remaining tenements, the sombre-hued colony of Syrians is astir with preparation for the holiday. How comes it that in the only settlement of the real Christmas people in New York the corner saloon appropriates to itself all the outward signs of it? Even the floral cross that is nailed over the door of the Orthodox church is long withered and dead; it has been there since Easter, and it is yet twelve days to Christmas by the belated reckoning of the Greek Church. But if the houses show no sign of the holiday, within there is nothing lacking. The whole colony is gone a-visiting. There are enough of the unorthodox to set the fashion, and the rest follow the custom of the country. The men go from house to house, shake hands, and kiss one another on both cheeks, with the salutation, "Kol am va antom Salimoon." "Every year and you are safe," the Syrian guide renders it into English; and a non-professional interpreter amends it: "May you grow happier year by year." Arrack made from grapes and flavored with aniseseed, and candy baked in little white balls like marbles, are served with the indispensable cigarette; for long callers, the pipe.

In a top-floor room of one of the darkest of the dilapidated tenements, the dusty window panes of which the last glow in the winter sky is tinging faintly with red, a dance is in progress. The guests, most of them fresh from the hillsides of Mount Lebanon, squat about the room. A reed-pipe and a tambourine furnish the music. One has the centre of the floor. With a beer jug filled to the brim on his head, he skips and sways, bending, twisting, kneeling, gesturing, and keeping time, while the men clap their hands. He lies down and turns over, but not a drop is spilled. Another succeeds him, stepping proudly, gracefully, furling and unfurling a handkerchief like a banner. As he sits down, and the beer goes around, one in the corner, who looks like a shepherd fresh from his pasture, strikes up a song—a far-off, lonesome, plaintive lay. "Far as the hills," says the guide; "a song of the old days and the old people, now seldom heard." All together croon the refrain. The host delivers himself of an epic about his love across the seas, with the most agonizing expression, and in a shockingly bad voice. He is the worst singer I ever heard; but his companions greet his effort with approving shouts of "Yi! yi!" They look so fierce, and yet are so childishly happy, that at the thought of their exile and of the dark tenement the question arises, "Why all this joy?" The guide answers it with a look of surprise. "They sing," he says, "because they are glad they are free. Did you not know?"

The bells in old Trinity chime the midnight hour. From dark hallways men and women pour forth and hasten to the Maronite church. In the loft of the dingy old warehouse wax candles burn before an altar of brass. The priest, in a white robe with a huge gold cross worked on the back, chants the ritual. The people respond. The women kneel in the aisles, shrouding their heads in their shawls; a surpliced acolyte swings his censer; the heavy perfume of burning incense fills the hall.

The band at the anarchists' ball is tuning up for the last dance. Young and old float to the happy strains, forgetting injustice, oppression, hatred. Children slide upon the waxed floor, weaving fearlessly in and out between the couples—between fierce, bearded men and short-haired women with crimson-bordered kerchiefs. A Punch-and-Judy show in the corner evokes shouts of laughter.

Outside the snow is falling. It sifts silently into each nook and corner, softens all the hard and ugly lines, and throws the spotless mantle of charity over the blemishes, the shortcomings. Christmas morning will dawn pure and white.

WHAT THE CHRISTMAS SUN SAW IN THE TENEMENTS

The December sun shone clear and cold upon the city. It shone upon rich and poor alike. It shone into the homes of the wealthy on the avenues and in the up-town streets, and into courts and alleys hedged in by towering tenements down town. It shone upon throngs of busy holiday shoppers that went out and in at the big stores, carrying bundles big and small, all alike filled with Christmas cheer and kindly messages from Santa Claus.

It shone down so gayly and altogether cheerily there, that wraps and overcoats were unbuttoned for the north wind to toy with. "My, isn't it a nice day?" said one young lady in a fur shoulder cape to a friend, pausing to kiss and compare lists of Christmas gifts.

"Most too hot," was the reply, and the friends passed on. There was warmth within and without. Life was very pleasant under the Christmas sun up on the avenue.

Down in Cherry Street the rays of the sun climbed over a row of tall tenements with an effort that seemed to exhaust all the life that was in them, and fell into a dirty block, half choked with trucks, with ash barrels and rubbish of all sorts, among which the dust was whirled in clouds upon fitful, shivering blasts that searched every nook and cranny of the big barracks. They fell upon a little girl, barefooted and in rags, who struggled out of an alley with a broken pitcher in her grimy fist, against the wind that set down the narrow slit like the draught through a big

WHAT THE CHRISTMAS SUN SAW IN THE TENEMENTS

factory chimney. Just at the mouth of the alley it took her with a sudden whirl, a cyclone of dust and drifting ashes, tossed her fairly off her feet, tore from her grip the threadbare shawl she clutched at her throat, and set her down at the saloon door breathless and half smothered. She had just time to dodge through the storm-doors before another whirlwind swept whistling down the street.

"My, but isn't it cold?" she said, as she shook the dust out of her shawl and set the pitcher down on the bar. "Gimme a pint," laying down a few pennies that had been wrapped in a corner of the shawl, "and mamma says make it good and full."

"All'us the way with youse kids—want a barrel when yees pays fer a pint," growled the bartender. "There, run along, and don't ye hang around that stove no more. We ain't a steam-heatin' the block fer nothin'."

The little girl clutched her shawl and the pitcher, and slipped out into the street where the wind lay in ambush and promptly bore down on her in pillars of whirling dust as soon as she appeared. But the sun that pitied her bare feet and little frozen hands played a trick on old Boreas—it showed her a way between the pillars, and only just her skirt was caught by one and whirled over her head as she dodged into her alley. It peeped after her halfway down its dark depths, where it seemed colder even than in the bleak street, but there it had to leave her.

It did not see her dive through the doorless opening into a hall where no sun-ray had ever entered. It could not have found its way in there had it tried. But up the narrow, squeaking stairs the girl with the pitcher was climbing. Up one flight of stairs, over a knot of children, half babies, pitching pennies on the landing, over wash-tubs and bedsteads that encumbered the next—house-cleaning going on in that "flat"; that is to say, the surplus of bugs was being turned out with petroleum and a feather—up still another, past a half-open door through which came the noise of brawling and curses. She dodged and quickened her step a little until she stood panting before a door on the fourth landing that opened readily as she pushed it with her bare foot.

A room almost devoid of stick or rag one might dignify with the name of furniture. Two chairs, one with a broken back, the other on three legs, beside a rickety table that stood upright only by leaning against the wall. On the unwashed floor a heap of straw covered with dirty bedtick for a bed; a foul-smelling slop-pail in the middle of the room; a crazy stove, and back of it a door or gap opening upon darkness. There was something in there, but what it was could only be surmised from a heavy snore that rose and fell regularly. It was the bedroom of the apartment, windowless, airless, and sunless, but rented at a price a millionaire would denounce as robbery.

"That you, Liza?" said a voice that discovered a woman bending over the stove. "Run 'n' get the childer. Dinner's ready."

The winter sun glancing down the wall of the opposite tenement, with a hopeless effort to cheer the back yard, might have peeped through the one window of the room in Mrs. McGroarty's "flat," had that window not been coated with the dust of ages, and discovered that dinner party in action. It might have found a score like it in the alley. Four unkempt children, copies each in his or her way of Liza and their mother, Mrs. McGroarty, who "did washing" for a living. A meat bone, a "cut" from the butcher's at four cents a pound, green pickles, stale bread and beer. Beer for the four, a sup all round, the baby included. Why not? It was the one relish the searching ray would have found there. Potatoes were there, too —potatoes and meat! Say not the poor in the tenements are starving. In New York only those starve who cannot get work and have not the courage to beg. Fifty thousand always out of a job, say those who pretend to know. A round half-million asking and getting charity in eight years, say the statisticians of the Charity Organization. Any one can go round and see for himself that no one need starve in New York.

From across the yard the sunbeam, as it crept up the wall, fell slantingly through the attic window whence issued the sound of hammer-blows. A man with a hard face stood in its light, driving nails into the lid of a soap box that was partly filled with straw. Something else was there; as he shifted the lid that didn't fit, the glimpse of sunshine fell across it; it was a dead child, a little baby in a white slip, bedded in straw in a soap box for a coffin. The man was hammering down the lid to take it to the Potter's Field. At the bed knelt the mother, dry-eyed, delirious from starvation that had killed her child. Five hungry, frightened children cowered in the corner, hardly daring to whisper as they looked from the father to the mother in terror.

There was a knock on the door that was drowned once, twice, in the noise of the hammer on the little coffin. Then it was opened gently, and a young woman came in with a basket. A little silver cross shone upon her breast. She went to the poor mother, and, putting her hand soothingly on her head, knelt by her with gentle and loving words. The half-crazed woman listened with averted face, then suddenly burst into tears and hid her throbbing head in the other's lap.

WHAT THE CHRISTMAS SUN SAW IN THE TENEMENTS

The man stopped hammering and stared fixedly upon the two; the children gathered around with devouring looks as the visitor took from her basket bread, meat, and tea. Just then, with a parting wistful look into the bare attic room, the sun-ray slipped away, lingered for a moment about the coping outside, and fled over the housetops.

As it sped on its winter-day journey, did it shine into any cabin in an Irish bog more desolate than these Cherry Street "homes"? An army of thousands, whose one bright and wholesome memory, only tradition of home, is that poverty-stricken cabin in the desolate bog, are herded in such barracks to-day in New York. Potatoes they have; yes, and meat at four cents—even seven. Beer for a relish—never without beer. But home? The home that was home, even in a bog, with the love of it that has made Ireland immortal and a tower of strength in the midst of her suffering—what of that? There are no homes in New York's poor tenements.

Down the crooked path of the Mulberry Street Bend the sunlight slanted into the heart of New York's Italy. It shone upon bandannas and yellow neckerchiefs; upon swarthy faces and corduroy breeches; upon black-haired girls—mothers at thirteen; upon hosts of bow-legged children rolling in the dirt; upon pedlers' carts and rag-pickers staggering under burdens that threatened to crush them at every step. Shone upon unnumbered Pasquales dwelling, working, idling, and gambling there. Shone upon the filthiest and foulest of New York's tenements, upon Bandits' Roost, upon Bottle Alley, upon the hidden byways that lead to the tramps' burrows. Shone upon the scene of annual infant slaughter. Shone into the foul core of New York's slums that was at last to go to the realm of bad memories because civilized man might not look upon it and live without blushing.

It glanced past the rag-shop in the cellar, whence welled up stenches to poison the town, into an apartment three flights up that held two women, one young, the other old and bent. The young one had a baby at her breast. She was rocking it tenderly in her arms, singing in the soft Italian tongue a lullaby, while the old granny listened eagerly, her elbows on her knees, and a stumpy clay pipe, blackened with age, between her teeth. Her eyes were set on the wall, on which the musty paper hung in tatters, fit frame for the wretched, poverty-stricken room, but they saw neither poverty nor want; her aged limbs felt not the cold draught from without, in which they shivered; she looked far over the seas to sunny Italy, whose music was in her ears.

"O dolce Napoli," she mumbled between her toothless jaws, "O suol beato——"

The song ended in a burst of passionate grief. The old granny and the baby woke up at once. They were not in sunny Italy; not under southern, cloudless skies. They were in "The Bend," in Mulberry Street, and the wintry wind rattled the door as if it would say, in the language of their new home, the land of the free: "Less music! More work! Root, hog, or die!"

Around the corner the sunbeam danced with the wind into Mott Street, lifted the blouse of a Chinaman and made it play tag with his pigtail. It used him so roughly that he was glad to skip from it down a cellar-way that gave out fumes of opium strong enough to scare even the north wind from its purpose. The soles of his felt shoes showed as he disappeared down the ladder that passed for cellar steps. Down there, where daylight never came, a group of yellow, almond-eyed men were bending over a table playing fan-tan. Their very souls were in the game, every faculty of the mind bent on the issue and the stake. The one blouse that was indifferent to what went on was stretched on a mat in a corner. One end of a clumsy pipe was in his mouth, the other held over a little spirit-lamp on the divan on which he lay. Something fluttered in the flame with a pungent, unpleasant smell. The smoker took a long draught, inhaling the white smoke, then sank back on his couch in senseless content.

Upstairs tiptoed the noiseless felt shoes, bent on some house errand, to the "household" floors above, where young white girls from the tenements of The Bend and the East Side live in slavery worse, if not more galling, than any of the galley with ball and chain—the slavery of the pipe. Four, eight, sixteen, twenty-odd such "homes" in this tenement, disgracing the very name of home and family, for marriage and troth are not in the bargain.

In one room, between the half-drawn curtains of which the sunbeam works its way in, three girls are lying on as many bunks, smoking all. They are very young, "under age," though each and every one would glibly swear in court to the satisfaction of the police that she is sixteen, and therefore free to make her own bad choice. Of these, one was brought up among the rugged hills of Maine; the other two are from the tenement crowds, hardly missed there. But their companion? She is twirling the sticky brown pill over the lamp, preparing to fill the bowl of her pipe with it. As she does so, the sunbeam dances across the bed, kisses the red spot on her cheek that betrays the secret her tyrant long has known,—though to her it is hidden yet,—that the pipe has claimed its victim and soon will pass it on to the Potter's Field.

"Nell," says one of her chums in the other bunk, something stirred within her by the flash, "Nell, did you hear from the old farm to home since you come here?"

Nell turns half around, with the toasting-stick in her hand, an ugly look on her wasted features, a vile oath on her lips.

"To hell with the old farm," she says, and putting the pipe to her mouth inhales it all, every bit, in one long breath, then falls back on her pillow in drunken stupor.

That is what the sun of a winter day saw and heard in Mott Street.

It had travelled far toward the west, searching many dark corners and vainly seeking entry to others; had glided with equal impartiality the spires of five hundred churches and the tin cornices of thirty thousand tenements, with their million tenants and more; had smiled courage and cheer to patient mothers trying to make the most of life in the teeming crowds, that had too little sunshine by far; hope to toiling fathers striving early and late for bread to fill the many mouths clamoring to be fed.

The brief December day was far spent. Now its rays fell across the North River and lighted up the windows of the tenements in Hell's Kitchen and Poverty Gap. In the Gap especially they made a brave show; the windows of the crazy old frame-house under the big tree that sat back from the street looked as if they were made of beaten gold. But the glory did not cross the threshold. Within it was dark and dreary and cold. The room at the foot of the rickety, patched stairs was empty. The last tenant was beaten to death by her husband in his drunken fury. The sun's rays shunned the spot ever after, though it was long since it could have made out the red daub from the mould on the rotten floor.

Upstairs, in the cold attic, where the wind wailed mournfully through every open crack, a little girl sat sobbing as if her heart would break. She hugged an old doll to her breast. The paint was gone from its face; the yellow hair was in a tangle; its clothes hung in rags. But she only hugged it closer. It was her doll. They had been friends so long, shared hunger and hardship together, and now——

Her tears fell faster. One drop trembled upon the wan cheek of the doll. The last sunbeam shot athwart it and made it glisten like a priceless jewel. Its glory grew and filled the room. Gone were the black walls, the darkness, and the cold. There was warmth and light and joy. Merry voices and glad faces were all about. A flock of children danced with gleeful shouts about a great Christmas tree in the middle of the floor. Upon its branches hung drums and trumpets and toys, and countless candles gleamed like beautiful stars. Farthest up, at the very top, her doll, her very own, with arms outstretched, as if appealing to be taken down and hugged. She knew it, knew the mission-school that had seen her first and only real Christmas, knew the gentle face of her teacher, and the writing on the wall she had taught her to spell out: "In His name." His name, who, she had said, was all little children's friend. Was He also her dolly's friend, and would He know it among the strange people?

The light went out; the glory faded. The bare room, only colder and more cheerless than before, was left. The child shivered. Only that morning the doctor had told her mother that she must have medicine and food and warmth, or she must go to the great hospital where papa had gone before, when their money was all spent. Sorrow and want had laid the mother upon the bed he had barely left. Every stick of furniture, every stitch of clothing on which money could be borrowed, had gone to the pawnbroker. Last of all, she had carried mamma's wedding-ring to pay the druggist. Now there was no more left, and they had nothing to eat. In a little while mamma would wake up, hungry.

The little girl smothered a last sob and rose quickly. She wrapped the doll in a threadbare shawl as well as she could, tiptoed to the door, and listened a moment to the feeble breathing of the sick mother within. Then she went out, shutting the door softly behind her, lest she wake her.

Up the street she went, the way she knew so well, one block and a turn round the saloon corner, the sunset glow kissing the track of her bare feet in the snow as she went, to a door that rang a noisy bell as she opened it and went in. A musty smell filled the close room. Packages, great and small, lay piled high on shelves behind the worn counter. A slovenly woman was haggling with the pawnbroker about the money for a skirt she had brought to pledge.

"Not a cent more than a quarter," he said, contemptuously, tossing the garment aside. "It's half worn out it is, dragging it back and forth over the counter these six months. Take it or leave it. Hallo! What have we here? Little Finnegan, eh? Your mother not dead yet? It's in the poor-house ye will be if she lasts much longer. What the——"

He had taken the package from the trembling child's hand—the precious doll—and unrolled the shawl. A moment he stood staring in dumb amazement at its contents. Then he caught it up and flung it with an angry oath upon the floor, where it was shivered against the coal-box.

"Get out o' here, ye Finnegan brat," he shouted; "I'll tache ye to come a-guyin' o' me. I'll——"

The door closed with a bang upon the frightened child, alone in the cold night. The sun saw not its home-coming. It had hidden behind the night clouds, weary of the sight of man and his cruelty.

Evening had worn into night. The busy city slept. Down by the wharves, now deserted, a poor boy sat on the bulwark, hungry, foot-sore, and shivering with cold. He sat thinking of friends and home, thousands of miles away over the sea, whom he had left six months before to go among strangers. He had been alone ever since, but never more so than that night. His money gone, no work to be found, he had slept in the streets for nights. That day he had eaten nothing; he would rather die than beg, and one of the two he must do soon.

There was the dark river rushing at his feet; the swirl of the unseen waters whispered to him of rest and peace he had not known since—it was so cold—and who was there to care, he thought bitterly. No one would ever know. He moved a little nearer the edge, and listened more intently.

A low whine fell on his ear, and a cold, wet face was pressed against his. A little crippled dog that had been crouching silently beside him nestled in his lap. He had picked it up in the street, as forlorn and friendless as himself, and it had stayed by him. Its touch recalled him to himself. He got up hastily, and, taking the dog in his arms, went to the police station near by, and asked for shelter. It was the first time he had accepted even such charity, and as he lay down on his rough plank he hugged a little gold locket he wore around his neck, the last link with better days, and thought with a hard sob of home. In the middle of the night he awoke with a start. The locket was gone. One of the tramps who slept with him had stolen it. With bitter tears he went up and complained to the Sergeant at the desk, and the Sergeant ordered him to be kicked out into the street as a liar, if not a thief. How should a tramp boy have come honestly by a gold locket? The doorman put him out as he was bidden, and when the little dog showed its teeth, a policeman seized it and clubbed it to death on the step.

WHAT THE CHRISTMAS SUN SAW IN THE TENEMENTS

Far from the slumbering city the rising moon shines over a wide expanse of glistening water. It silvers the snow upon a barren heath between two shores, and shortens with each passing minute the shadows of countless headstones that bear no names, only numbers. The breakers that beat against the bluff wake not those who sleep there. In the deep trenches they lie, shoulder to shoulder, an army of brothers, homeless in life, but here at rest and at peace. A great cross stands upon the lonely shore. The moon sheds its rays upon it in silent benediction and floods the garden of the unknown, unmourned dead with its soft light. Out on the Sound the fishermen see it flashing white against the starlit sky, and bare their heads reverently as their boats speed by, borne upon the wings of the west wind.

NIBSY'S CHRISTMAS

It was Christmas Eve over on the East Side. Darkness was closing in on a cold, hard day. The light that struggled through the frozen windows of the delicatessen store and the saloon on the corner, fell upon men with empty dinner-pails who were hurrying homeward, their coats buttoned tightly, and heads bent against the steady blast from the river, as if they were butting their way down the street.

The wind had forced the door of the saloon ajar, and was whistling through the crack; but in there it seemed to make no one afraid. Between roars of laughter, the clink of glasses and the rattle of dice on the hardwood counter were heard out in the street. More than one of the passers-by who came within range was taken with an extra shiver in which the vision of wife and little ones waiting at home for his coming was snuffed out, as he dropped in to brace up. The lights were long out when the silent streets reëchoed his unsteady steps toward home, where the Christmas welcome had turned to dread.

But in this twilight hour they burned brightly yet, trying hard to pierce the bitter cold outside with a ray of warmth and cheer. Where the lamps in the delicatessen store made a mottled streak of brightness across the flags, two little boys stood with their noses flattened against the window. The warmth inside, and the lights, had made little islands of clear space on the frosty pane, affording glimpses of the wealth within, of the piles of smoked herring, of golden cheese, of sliced bacon and generous, fat-bellied hams; of the rows of odd-shaped bottles and jars on the shelves that held there was no telling what good things, only it was certain that they must be good from the looks of them.

And the heavenly smell of spices and things that reached the boys through the open door each time the tinkling bell announced the coming or going of a customer! Better than all, back there on the top shelf the stacks of square honey-cakes, with their frosty coats of sugar, tied in bundles with strips of blue paper.

The wind blew straight through the patched and threadbare jackets of the lads as they crept closer to the window, struggling hard by breathing on the pane to make their peep-holes bigger, to take in the whole of the big cake with the almonds set in; but they did not heed it.

"Jim!" piped the smaller of the two, after a longer stare than usual; "hey, Jim! them's Sante Claus's. See 'em?"

"Sante Claus!" snorted the other, scornfully, applying his eye to the clear spot on the pane. "There ain't no ole duffer like dat. Them's honey-cakes. Me 'n' Tom had a bite o' one wunst."

"There ain't no Sante Claus?" retorted the smaller shaver, hotly, at his peep-hole. "There is, too. I seen him myself when he cum to our alley last——"

"What's youse kids a-scrappin' fur?" broke in a strange voice.

Another boy, bigger, but dirtier and tougher-looking than either of the two, had come up behind them unobserved. He carried an armful of unsold "extras" under one arm. The other was buried to the elbow in the pocket of his ragged trousers.

The "kids" knew him, evidently, and the smallest eagerly accepted him as umpire.

"It's Jim w'at says there ain't no Sante Claus, and I seen him——"

"Jim!" demanded the elder ragamuffin, sternly, looking hard at the culprit; "Jim! yere a chump! No Sante Claus? What're ye givin' us? Now, watch me!"

With utter amazement the boys saw him disappear through the door under the tinkling bell into the charmed precincts of smoked herring, jam, and honey-cakes. Petrified at their peep-holes, they watched him, in the veritable presence of Santa Claus himself with the fir-branch, fish out five battered pennies from the depths of his pocket and pass them over to the woman behind the jars, in exchange for one of the bundles of honey-cakes tied with blue. As if in a dream they saw him issue forth with the coveted prize.

"There, kid!" he said, holding out the two fattest and whitest cakes to Santa Claus's champion; "there's yer Christmas. Run along, now, to yer barracks; and you, Jim, here's one for you, though yer don't desarve it. Mind ye let the kid alone."

"This one'll have to do for me grub, I guess. I ain't sold me 'Newses,' and the ole man'll kick if I bring 'em home."

Before the shuffling feet of the ragamuffins hurrying homeward had turned the corner, the last mouthful of the newsboy's supper was smothered in a yell of "Extree!" as he shot across the street to intercept a passing stranger.

As the evening wore on, it grew rawer and more blustering still. Flakes of dry snow that stayed where they fell, slowly tracing the curb-lines, the shutters, and the doorsteps of the tenements with gathering white, were borne up on the storm from the water. To the right and left stretched endless streets between the towering barracks, as beneath frowning cliffs pierced with a thousand glowing eyes that revealed the watch-fires within —a mighty city of cave-dwellers held in the thraldom of poverty and want.

Outside there was yet hurrying to and fro. Saloon doors were slamming, and bare-legged urchins, carrying beer-jugs, hugged the walls close for shelter. From the depths of a blind alley floated out the discordant strains of a vagabond brass band "blowing in" the yule of the poor. Banished by police ordinance from the street, it reaped a scant harvest of pennies for Christmas cheer from the windows opening on the back yard. Against more than one pane showed the bald outline of a forlorn little Christmas tree, some stray branch of a hemlock picked up at the grocer's and set in a pail for "the childer" to dance around, a dime's worth of candy and tinsel on the boughs.

From the attic over the way came, in spells between, the gentle tones of a German song about the Christ-child. Christmas in the East Side tenements begins with the sunset on the "Holy Eve," except where the name is as a threat or a taunt. In a hundred such homes the whir of many sewing-machines, worked by the sweater's slaves with weary feet and aching backs, drowned every feeble note of joy that struggled to make itself heard above the noise of the great treadmill.

To these what was Christmas but the name for suffering, reminder of lost kindred and liberty, or the slavery of eighteen hundred years, freedom from which was purchased only with gold. Ay, gold! The gold that had power to buy freedom yet, to buy the good-will, ay, and the good name, of the oppressor, with his houses and land. At the thought the tired eye glistened, the aching back straightened, and to the weary foot there came new strength to finish the long task while the city slept.

Where a narrow passageway put in between two big tenements to a ramshackle rear barrack, Nibsy, the newsboy, halted in the shadow of the doorway and stole a long look down the dark alley.

He toyed uncertainly with his still unsold papers—worn dirty and ragged as his clothes by this time—before he ventured in, picking his way between barrels and heaps of garbage; past the Italian cobbler's hovel, where a tallow dip, stuck in a cracked beer-glass, before a picture of the "Mother of God," showed that even he knew it was Christmas and liked to show it; past the Sullivan flat, where blows and drunken curses mingled with the shriek of women, as Nibsy had heard many nights before this one.

He shuddered as he felt his way past the door, partly with a premonition of what was in store for himself, if the "old man" was at home, partly with a vague, uncomfortable feeling that somehow Christmas Eve should be different from other nights, even in the alley; down to its farthest end, to the last rickety flight of steps that led into the filth and darkness of the tenement. Up this he crept, three flights, to a door at which he stopped and listened, hesitating, as he had stopped at the entrance to the alley; then, with a sudden, defiant gesture, he pushed it open and went in.

A bare and cheerless room; a pile of rags for a bed in the corner, another in the dark alcove, miscalled bedroom; under the window a broken candle and an iron-bound chest, upon which sat a sad-eyed woman with hard lines in her face, peeling potatoes in a pan; in the middle of the room a rusty stove, with a pile of wood, chopped on the floor alongside. A man on his knees in front fanning the fire with an old slouch hat. With each breath of draught he stirred; the crazy old pipe belched forth torrents of smoke at every joint. As Nibsy entered, the man desisted from his efforts and sat up, glaring at him—a villainous ruffian's face, scowling with anger.

"Late ag'in!" he growled; "an' yer papers not sold. What did I tell yer, brat, if ye dared——"

"Tom! Tom!" broke in the wife, in a desperate attempt to soothe the ruffian's temper. "The boy can't help it, an' it's Christmas Eve. For the love o'——"

"The devil take yer rot and yer brat!" shouted the man, mad with the

NIBSY'S CHRISTMAS

fury of passion. "Let me at him!" and, reaching over, he seized a heavy knot of wood and flung it at the head of the boy.

Nibsy had remained just inside the door, edging slowly toward his mother, but with a watchful eye on the man at the stove. At the first movement of his hand toward the woodpile he sprang for the stairway with the agility of a cat, and just dodged the missile. It struck the door, as he slammed it behind him, with force enough to smash the panel.

Down the three flights in as many jumps he went, and through the alley, over barrels and barriers, never stopping once till he reached the street, and curses and shouts were left behind.

In his flight he had lost his unsold papers, and he felt ruefully in his pocket as he went down the street, pulling his rags about him as much from shame as to keep out the cold.

Four pennies were all he had left after his Christmas treat to the two little lads from the barracks; not enough for supper or for a bed; and it was getting colder all the time.

On the sidewalk in front of the notion store a belated Christmas party was in progress. The children from the tenements in the alley and across the way were having a game of blind-man's-buff, groping blindly about in the crowd to catch each other. They hailed Nibsy with shouts of laughter, calling to him to join in.

"We're having Christmas!" they yelled.

Nibsy did not hear them. He was thinking, thinking, the while turning over his four pennies at the bottom of his pocket. Thinking if Christmas was ever to come to him, and the children's Santa Claus to find his alley where the baby slept within reach of her father's cruel hand. As for him, he had never known anything but blows and curses. He could take care of himself. But his mother and the baby—And then it came to him with shuddering cold that it was getting late, and that he must find a place to sleep.

He weighed in his mind the merits of two or three places where he was in the habit of hiding from the "cops" when the alley got to be too hot for him.

There was the hay barge down by the dock, with the watchman who got drunk sometimes, and so gave the boys a chance. The chances were at least even of its being available on Christmas Eve, and of Santa Claus having thus done him a good turn after all.

Then there was the snug berth in the sand-box you could curl all up in. Nibsy thought with regret of its being, like the hay barge, so far away and to windward, too.

Down by the printing-offices there were the steam gratings, and a chance corner in the cellars, stories and stories underground, where the big presses keep up such a clatter from midnight till far into the day.

As he passed them in review, Nibsy made up his mind with sudden determination, and, setting his face toward the south, made off down town.

The rumble of the last departing news-wagon over the pavement, now buried deep in snow, had died away in the distance, when, from out of the bowels of the earth there issued a cry, a cry of mortal terror and pain that was echoed by a hundred throats.

From one of the deep cellar-ways a man ran out, his clothes and hair and beard afire; on his heels a breathless throng of men and boys; following them, close behind, a rush of smoke and fire.

The clatter of the presses ceased suddenly, to be followed quickly by the clangor of hurrying fire-bells. With hooks and axes the firemen rushed in; hose was let down through the manholes, and down there in the depths the battle was fought and won.

The building was saved; but in the midst of the rejoicing over the victory there fell a sudden silence. From the cellar-way a grimy, helmeted figure arose, with something black and scorched in his arms. A tarpaulin was spread upon the snow and upon it he laid his burden, while the silent crowd made room and word went over to the hospital for the doctor to come quickly.

Very gently they lifted poor little Nisby—for it was he, caught in his berth by a worse enemy than the "cop" or the watchman of the hay barge—into the ambulance that bore him off to the hospital cot, too late.

Conscious only of a vague discomfort that had succeeded terror and pain, Nibsy wondered uneasily why they were all so kind. Nobody had taken the trouble to as much as notice him before. When he had thrust his papers into their very faces they had pushed him roughly aside.

Nibsy, unhurt and able to fight his way, never had a show. Sick and maimed and sore, he was being made much of, though he had been caught where the boys were forbidden to go. Things were queer, anyhow, and——

NIBSY'S CHRISTMAS

The room was getting so dark that he could hardly see the doctor's kindly face, and had to grip his hand tightly to make sure that he was there; almost as dark as the stairs in the alley he had come down in such a hurry.

There was the baby now—poor baby—and mother—and then a great blank, and it was all a mystery to poor Nibsy no longer. For, just as a wild-eyed woman pushed her way through the crowd of nurses and doctors to his bedside, crying for her boy, Nibsy gave up his soul to God.

It was very quiet in the alley. Christmas had come and gone. Upon the last door a bow of soiled crape was nailed up with two tacks. It had done duty there a dozen times before, that year.

Upstairs, Nibsy was at home, and for once the neighbors, one and all, old and young, came to see him.

Even the father, ruffian that he was, offered no objection. Cowed and silent, he sat in the corner by the window farthest from where the plain little coffin stood, with the lid closed down.

A couple of the neighbor-women were talking in low tones by the stove, when there came a timid knock at the door. Nobody answering, it was pushed open, first a little, then far enough to admit the shrinking form of a little ragamuffin, the smaller of the two who had stood breathing peep-holes on the window pane of the delicatessen store the night before when Nibsy came along.

He dragged with him a hemlock branch, the leavings from some Christmas tree at the grocery.

"It's from Sante Claus," he said, laying it on the coffin. "Nibsy knows." And he went out.

Santa Claus had come to Nibsy, after all, in his alley. And Nibsy knew.

THE LITTLE DOLLAR'S CHRISTMAS JOURNEY

"It is too bad," said Mrs. Lee, and she put down the magazine in which she had been reading of the poor children in the tenements of the great city that know little of Christmas joys; "no Christmas tree! One of them shall have one, at any rate. I think this will buy it, and it is so handy to send. Nobody would know that there was money in the letter." And she enclosed a coupon in a letter to a professor, a friend in the city, who, she knew, would have no trouble in finding the child, and had it mailed at once. Mrs. Lee was a widow whose not too great income was derived from the interest on some four per cent government bonds which represented the savings of her husband's life of toil, that was none the less hard because it was spent in a counting-room and not with shovel and spade. The coupon looked for all the world like a dollar bill, except that it was so small that a baby's hand could easily cover it. The United States, the printing on it said, would pay on demand to the bearer one dollar; and there was a number on it, just as on a full-grown dollar, that was the number of the bond from which it had been cut.

The letter travelled all night, and was tossed and sorted and bunched at the end of its journey in the great gray beehive that never sleeps, day or night, and where half the tears and joys of the land, including this account of the little dollar, are checked off unceasingly as first-class matter or second or third, as the case may be. In the morning it was laid, none the worse for its journey, at the professor's breakfast plate. The professor was a kindly man, and he smiled as he read it. "To procure one small Christmas tree for a poor tenement," was its errand.

"Little dollar," he said, "I think I know where you are needed." And he made a note in his book. There were other notes there that made him smile again as he saw them. They had names set opposite them. One about a Noah's ark was marked "Vivi." That was the baby; and there was one about a doll's carriage that had the words "Katie, sure," set over against it. The professor eyed the list in mock dismay.

"How ever will I do it?" he sighed, as he put on his hat.

"Well, you will have to get Santa Claus to help you, John," said his wife, buttoning his greatcoat about him. "And, mercy! the duckses' babies! don't forget them, whatever you do. The baby has been talking about nothing else since he saw them at the store, the old duck and the two ducklings on wheels. You know them, John?"

But the professor was gone, repeating to himself as he went down the garden walk, "The duckses' babies, indeed!" He chuckled as he said it, why I cannot tell. He was very particular about his grammar, was the professor, ordinarily. Perhaps it was because it was Christmas Eve.

Down town went the professor; but instead of going with the crowd that was setting toward Santa Claus's headquarters, in the big Broadway store, he turned off into a quieter street, leading west. It took him to a narrow thoroughfare, with five-story tenements frowning on their side, where the people he met were not so well dressed as those he had left behind, and did not seem to be in such a hurry of joyful anticipation of the holiday. Into one of the tenements he went, and, groping his way through a pitch-dark hall, came to a door way back, the last one to the left, at which he knocked. An expectant voice said, "Come in," and the professor pushed open the door.

The room was very small, very stuffy, and very dark, so dark that a smoking kerosene lamp that burned on a table next the stove hardly lighted it at all, though it was broad day. A big, unshaven man, who sat on the bed, rose when he saw the visitor, and stood uncomfortably shifting his feet and avoiding the professor's eye. The latter's glance was serious, though not unkind, as he asked the woman with the baby if he had found no work yet.

"No," she said, anxiously coming to the rescue, "not yet; he was waitin' for a recommend." But Johnnie had earned two dollars running errands, and, now there was a big fall of snow, his father might get a job of shovelling. The woman's face was worried, yet there was a cheerful note in her voice that somehow made the place seem less discouraging than it was. The baby she nursed was not much larger than a middle-sized doll. Its little face looked thin and wan. It had been very sick, she explained, but the doctor said it was mending now. That was good, said the professor, and patted one of the bigger children on the head.

There were six of them, of all sizes, from Johnnie, who could run errands, down. They were busy fixing up a Christmas tree that half filled the room, though it was of the very smallest. Yet, it was a real Christmas tree, left over from the Sunday-school stock, and it was dressed up at that. Pictures from the colored supplement of a Sunday newspaper hung and stood on every branch, and three pieces of colored glass, suspended on threads that shone in the smoky lamplight, lent color and real beauty to the show. The children were greatly tickled.

"John put it up," said the mother, by way of explanation, as the professor eyed it approvingly. "There ain't nothing to eat on it. If there was, it wouldn't be there a minute. The childer be always a-searchin' in it."

"But there must be, or else it isn't a real Christmas tree," said the professor, and brought out the little dollar. "This is a dollar which a friend gave me for the children's Christmas, and she sends her love with it. Now, you buy them some things and a few candles, Mrs. Ferguson, and then a good supper for the rest of the family. Good night, and a Merry Christmas to you. I think myself the baby is getting better." It had just opened its eyes and laughed at the tree.

The professor was not very far on his way toward keeping his appointment with Santa Claus before Mrs. Ferguson was at the grocery laying in her dinner. A dollar goes a long way when it is the only one in the house; and when she had everything, including two cents' worth of flitter-gold, four apples, and five candles for the tree, the grocer footed up her bill on the bag that held her potatoes—ninety-eight cents. Mrs. Ferguson gave him the little dollar.

"What's this?" said the grocer, his fat smile turning cold as he laid a restraining hand on the full basket. "That ain't no good."

"It's a dollar, ain't it?" said the woman, in alarm. "It's all right. I know the man that give it to me."

"It ain't all right in this store," said the grocer, sternly. "Put them things back. I want none o' that."

The woman's eyes filled with tears as she slowly took the lid off the basket and lifted out the precious bag of potatoes. They were waiting for that dinner at home. The children were even then camping on the doorstep to take her in to the tree in triumph. And now——

For the second time a restraining hand was laid upon her basket; but this time it was not the grocer's. A gentleman who had come in to order a Christmas turkey had overheard the conversation, and had seen the strange bill.

"It is all right," he said to the grocer. "Give it to me. Here is a dollar bill for it of the kind you know. If all your groceries were as honest as this bill, Mr. Schmidt, it would be a pleasure to trade with you. Don't be afraid to trust Uncle Sam where you see his promise to pay."

The gentleman held the door open for Mrs. Ferguson, and heard the shout of the delegation awaiting her on the stoop as he went down the street.

"I wonder where that came from, now," he mused. "Coupons in Bedford Street! I suppose somebody sent it to the woman for a Christmas gift. Hello! Here are old Thomas and Snowflake. Now, wouldn't it surprise her old stomach if I gave her a Christmas gift of oats? If only the shock doesn't kill her! Thomas! Oh, Thomas!"

The old man thus hailed stopped and awaited the gentleman's coming. He was a cartman who did odd jobs through the ward, so picking up a living for himself and the white horse, which the boys had dubbed Snowflake in a spirit of fun. They were a well-matched old pair, Thomas and his horse. One was not more decrepit than the other.

There was a tradition along the docks, where Thomas found a job now and then, and Snowflake an occasional straw to lunch on, that they were of an age, but this was denied by Thomas.

"See here," said the gentleman, as he caught up with them; "I want Snowflake to keep Christmas, Thomas. Take this and buy him a bag of oats. And give it to him carefully, do you hear?—not all at once, Thomas. He isn't used to it."

"Gee whizz!" said the old man, rubbing his eyes with his cap, as his friend passed out of sight, "oats fer Christmas! G'lang, Snowflake; yer in luck."

The feed-man put on his spectacles and looked Thomas over at the strange order. Then he scanned the little dollar, first on one side, then on the other.

"Never seed one like him," he said. "'Pears to me he is mighty short. Wait till I send round to the hockshop. He'll know, if anybody."

The man at the pawnshop did not need a second look. "Why, of course," he said, and handed a dollar bill over the counter. "Old Thomas, did you say? Well, I am blamed if the old man ain't got a stocking after all. They're a sly pair, he and Snowflake."

Business was brisk that day at the pawnshop. The door-bell tinkled early and late, and the stock on the shelves grew. Bundle was added to bundle. It had been a hard winter so far. Among the callers in the early afternoon was a young girl in a gingham dress and without other covering, who stood timidly at the counter and asked for three dollars on a watch, a keepsake evidently, which she was loath to part with. Perhaps it was the last glimpse of brighter days. The pawnbroker was doubtful; it was not worth so much. She pleaded hard, while he compared the number of the movement with a list sent in from Police Headquarters.

"Two," he said decisively at last, snapping the case shut—"two or nothing." The girl handed over the watch with a troubled sigh. He made out a ticket and gave it to her with a handful of silver change.

Was it the sigh and her evident distress, or was it the little dollar? As she turned to go, he called her back.

"Here, it is Christmas!" he said. "I'll run the risk." And he added the coupon to the little heap.

The girl looked at it and at him questioningly.

"It is all right," he said; "you can take it; I'm running short of change. Bring it back if they won't take it. I'm good for it." Uncle Sam had achieved a backer.

In Grand Street the holiday crowds jammed every store in their eager hunt for bargains. In one of them, at the knit-goods counter, stood the girl from the pawnshop, picking out a thick, warm shawl. She hesitated between a gray and a maroon-colored one, and held them up to the light.

"For you?" asked the salesgirl, thinking to aid her. She glanced at her thin dress and shivering form as she said it.

"No," said the girl; "for mother; she is poorly and needs it." She chose the gray, and gave the salesgirl her handful of money.

The girl gave back the coupon.

"They don't go," she said; "give me another, please."

"But I haven't got another," said the girl, looking apprehensively at the shawl. "The—Mr. Feeney said it was all right. Take it to the desk, please, and ask."

The salesgirl took the bill and the shawl, and went to the desk. She came back, almost immediately, with the storekeeper, who looked sharply at the customer and noted the number of the coupon.

"It is all right," he said, satisfied apparently by the inspection; "a little unusual, only. We don't see many of them. Can I help you, miss?" And he attended her to the door.

In the street there was even more of a Christmas show going on than in the stores. Pedlers of toys, of mottoes, of candles, and of knickknacks of every description stood in rows along the curb, and were driving a lively trade. Their push-carts were decorated with fir branches—even whole Christmas trees. One held a whole cargo of Santa Clauses in a bower of green, each one with a cedar-bush in his folded arms, as a soldier carries his gun. The lights were blazing out in the stores, and the hucksters' torches were flaring at the corners. There was Christmas in the very air and Christmas in the storekeeper's till. It had been a very busy day. He thought of it with a satisfied nod as he stood a moment breathing the brisk air of the winter day, absently fingering the coupon the girl had paid for the shawl. A thin voice at his elbow said: "Merry Christmas, Mr. Stein! Here's yer paper."

It was the newsboy who left the evening papers at the door every night. The storekeeper knew him, and something about the struggle they had at home to keep the roof over their heads. Mike was a kind of protégé of his. He had helped to get him his route.

"Wait a bit, Mike," he said. "You'll be wanting your Christmas from me. Here's a dollar. It's just like yourself: it is small, but it is all right. You take it home and have a good time."

Was it the message with which it had been sent forth from far away in the country, or what was it? Whatever it was, it was just impossible for the little dollar to lie still in the pocket while there was want to be relieved, mouths to be filled, or Christmas lights to be lit. It just couldn't, and it didn't.

Mike stopped around the corner of Allen Street, and gave three whoops expressive of his approval of Mr. Stein; having done which, he sidled up to the first lighted window out of range to examine his gift. His enthusiasm changed to open-mouthed astonishment as he saw the little dollar. His jaw fell. Mike was not much of a scholar, and could not make out the inscription on the coupon; but he had heard of shinplasters as something they "had in the war," and he took this to be some sort of a ten-cent piece. The policeman on the block might tell. Just now he and Mike were hunk. They had made up a little difference they'd had, and if any one would know, the cop surely would. And off he went in search of him.

Mr. McCarthy pulled off his gloves, put his club under his arm, and studied the little dollar with contracted brow. He shook his head as he handed it back, and rendered the opinion that it was "some dom swindle that's ag'in the law." He advised Mike to take it back to Mr. Stein, and added, as he prodded him in an entirely friendly manner in the ribs with his locust, that if it had been the week before he might have "run him in" for having the thing in his possession. As it happened, Mr. Stein was busy and not to be seen, and Mike went home between hope and fear, with his doubtful prize.

There was a crowd at the door of the tenement, and Mike saw, before he had reached it, running, that it clustered about an ambulance that was backed up to the sidewalk. Just as he pushed his way through the throng it drove off, its clanging gong scattering the people right and left. A little girl sat weeping on the top step of the stoop. To her Mike turned for information.

"Susie, what's up?" he asked, confronting her with his armful of papers. "Who's got hurted?"

"It's papa," sobbed the girl. "He ain't hurted. He's sick, and he was took that bad he had to go, an' to-morrer is Christmas, an'—oh, Mike!"

It is not the fashion of Essex Street to slop over. Mike didn't. He just set his mouth to a whistle and took a turn down the hall to think. Susie was his chum. There were seven in her flat; in his only four, including two that made wages. He came back from his trip with his mind made up.

"Suse," he said, "come on in. You take this, Suse, see! an' let the kids have their Christmas. Mr. Stein give it to me. It's a little one, but if it ain't all right I'll take it back and get one that is good. Go on, now, Suse, you hear?" And he was gone.

There was a Christmas tree that night in Susie's flat, with candles and apples and shining gold, but the little dollar did not pay for it. That rested securely in the purse of the charity visitor who had come that afternoon, just at the right time, as it proved. She had heard the story of Mike and his sacrifice, and had herself given the children a one-dollar bill for the coupon. They had their Christmas, and a joyful one, too, for the lady went up to the hospital and brought back word that Susie's father would be all right with rest and care, which he was now getting. Mike came in and helped them "sack" the tree when the lady was gone. He gave three more whoops for Mr. Stein, three for the lady, and three for the hospital doctor to even things up. Essex Street was all right that night.

"Do you know, professor," said that learned man's wife, when, after supper, he had settled down in his easy-chair to admire the Noah's ark and the duckses' babies and the rest, all of which had arrived safely by express ahead of him and were waiting to be detailed to their appropriate stockings while the children slept—"do you know, I heard such a story of a little newsboy to-day. It was at the meeting of our district charity committee this evening. Miss Linder, our visitor, came right from the house." And she told the story of Mike and Susie.

"And I just got the little dollar bill to keep. Here it is." She took the coupon out of her purse and passed it to her husband.

"Eh! what?" said the professor, adjusting his spectacles and reading the number. "If here isn't my little dollar come back to me! Why, where have you been, little one? I left you in Bedford Street this morning, and here you come by way of Essex. Well, I declare!" And he told his wife how he had received it in a letter in the morning.

"John," she said, with a sudden impulse,—she didn't know, and neither did he, that it was the charm of the little dollar that was working again,—"John, I guess it is a sin to stop it. Jones's children won't have any Christmas tree, because they can't afford it. He told me so this morning when he fixed the furnace. And the baby is sick. Let us give them the little dollar. He is here in the kitchen now."

And they did; and the Joneses, and I don't know how many others, had a Merry Christmas because of the blessed little dollar that carried Christmas cheer and good luck wherever it went. For all I know, it may be going yet. Certainly it is a sin to stop it, and if any one has locked it up without knowing that he locked up the Christmas dollar, let him start it right out again. He can tell it easily enough. If he just looks at the number, that's the one.

LITTLE WILL'S MESSAGE

"It is that or starve, Captain. I can't get a job. God knows I've tried, but without a recommend, it's no use. I ain't no good at beggin'. And—and—there's the childer."

There was a desperate note in the man's voice that made the Captain turn and look sharply at him. A swarthy, strongly built man in a rough coat, and with that in his dark face which told that he had lived longer than his years, stood at the door of the Detective Office. His hand that gripped the door handle shook so that the knob rattled in his grasp, but not with fear. He was no stranger to that place. Black Bill's face had looked out from the Rogues' Gallery longer than most of those now there could remember. The Captain looked him over in silence.

"You had better not, Bill," he said. "You know what will come of it. When you go up again it will be the last time. And up you go, sure."

The man started to say something, but choked it down and went out without a word. The Captain got up and rang his bell.

"Bill, who was here just now, is off again," he said to the officer who came to the door. "He says it is steal or starve, and he can't get a job. I guess he is right. Who wants a thief in his pay? And how can I recommend him? And still I think he would keep straight if he had the chance. Tell Murphy to look after him and see what he is up to."

The Captain went out, tugging viciously at his gloves. He was in very

LITTLE WILL'S MESSAGE

bad humor. The policeman at the Mulberry Street door got hardly a nod for his cheery "Merry Christmas" as he passed.

"Wonder what's crossed him," he said, looking down the street after him.

The green lamps were lighted and shone upon the hurrying six o'clock crowds from the Broadway shops. In the great business buildings the iron shutters were pulled down and the lights put out, and in a little while the reporters' boys that carried slips from Headquarters to the newspaper offices across the street were the only tenants of the block. A stray policeman stopped now and then on the corner and tapped the lamp-post reflectively with his club as he looked down the deserted street and wondered, as his glance rested upon the Chief's darkened windows, how it felt to have six thousand dollars a year and every night off. In the Detective Office the Sergeant who had come in at roll-call stretched himself behind the desk and thought of home. The lights of a Christmas tree in the abutting Mott Street tenement shone through his window, and the laughter of children mingled with the tap of the toy drum. He pulled down the sash in order to hear better. As he did so, a strong draught swept his desk. The outer door slammed. Two detectives came in bringing a prisoner between them. A woman accompanied them.

The Sergeant pulled the blotter toward him mechanically and dipped his pen.

"What's the charge?" he asked.

"Picking pockets in Fourteenth Street. This lady is the complainant, Mrs. ——"

The name was that of a well-known police magistrate. The Sergeant looked up and bowed. His glance took in the prisoner, and a look of recognition came into his face.

"What, Bill! So soon?" he said.

The prisoner was sullenly silent. He answered the questions put to him briefly, and was searched. The stolen pocket-book, a small paper package, and a crumpled letter were laid upon the desk. The Sergeant saw only the pocket-book.

"Looks bad," he said with wrinkled brow.

"We caught him at it," explained the officer. "Guess Bill has lost heart. He didn't seem to care. Didn't even try to get away."

The prisoner was taken to a cell. Silence fell once more upon the office. The Sergeant made a few red lines in the blotter and resumed his reveries. He was not in a mood for work. He hitched his chair nearer the

LITTLE WILL'S MESSAGE

window and looked across the yard. But the lights there were put out, the children's laughter had died away. Out of sorts at he hardly knew what, he leaned back in his chair, with his hands under the back of his head. Here it was Christmas Eve, and he at the desk instead of being out with the old woman buying things for the children. He thought with a sudden pang of conscience of the sled he had promised to get for Johnnie and had forgotten. That was hard luck. And what would Katie say when——

He had got that far when his eye, roaming idly over the desk, rested upon the little package taken from the thief's pocket. Something about it seemed to move him with sudden interest. He sat up and reached for it. He felt it carefully all over. Then he undid the package slowly and drew forth a woolly sheep. It had a blue ribbon about its neck, with a tiny bell hung on it.

The Sergeant set the sheep upon the desk and looked at it fixedly for better than a minute. Having apparently studied out its mechanism, he pulled its head and it baa-ed. He pulled it once more, and nodded. Then he took up the crumpled letter and opened it.

This was what he read, scrawled in a child's uncertain hand:—

"Deer Sante Claas—Pease wont yer bring me a sjeep wat bas. Aggie had won wonst. An Kate wants a dollie offul. In the reere 718 19th Street by the gas house. Your friend Will."

The Sergeant read it over twice very carefully and glanced over the page at the sheep, as if taking stock and wondering why Kate's dollie was not there. Then he took the sheep and the letter and went over to the Captain's door. A gruff "Come in!" answered his knock. The Captain was pulling off his overcoat. He had just come in from his dinner.

"Captain," said the Sergeant, "we found this in the pocket of Black Bill who is locked up for picking Mrs. ——'s pocket an hour ago. It is a clear case. He didn't even try to give them the slip," and he set the sheep upon the table and laid the letter beside it.

"Black Bill?" said the Captain, with something of a start; "the dickens you say!" And he took up the letter and read it. He was not a very good penman, was little Will. The Captain had even a harder time of it than the Sergeant had had making out his message. Three times he went over it, spelling out the words, and each time comparing it with the woolly exhibit that was part of the evidence, before he seemed to understand. Then it was in a voice that would have frightened little Will very much could he have heard it, and with a black look under his bushy eyebrows, that he bade the Sergeant "Fetch Bill up here!" One might almost have expected the little white lamb to have taken to its heels with fright at having raised such a storm, could it have run at all. But it showed no signs of fear. On the contrary it baa-ed quite lustily when the Sergeant should have been safely out of earshot. The hand of the Captain had accidentally rested upon the woolly head in putting down the letter. But the Sergeant was not out of earshot. He heard it and grinned.

An iron door in the basement clanged and there were steps in the passageway. The doorman brought in Bill. He stood by the door, sullenly submissive. The Captain raised his head. It was in the shade.

"So you are back, are you?" he said.

The thief nodded.

The Captain bent his brows upon him and said with sudden fierceness, "You couldn't keep honest a month, could you?"

"They wouldn't let me. Who wants a thief in his pay? And the children were starving."

It was said patiently enough, but it made the Captain wince all the same. They were his own words. But he did not give in so easily.

"Starving?" he repeated harshly. "And that's why you got this, I suppose," and he pushed the sheep from under the newspaper that had fallen upon it by accident and covered it up.

The thief looked at it and flushed to the temples. He tried to speak but could not. His face worked, and he seemed to be strangling. In the middle of his fight to master himself he saw the child's crumpled message on the desk. Taking a quick step across the room he snatched it up, wildly, fiercely.

"Captain," he gasped, and broke down utterly. The hardened thief wept like a woman.

The Captain rang his bell. He stood with his back to the prisoner when the doorman came in. "Take him down," he commanded. And the iron door clanged once more behind the prisoner.

Ten minutes later the reporters were discussing across the way the nature of "the case" which the night promised to develop. They had piped off the Captain and one of his trusted men leaving the building together, bound east. Could they have followed them all the way, they would have seen them get off the car at Nineteenth Street, and go toward the gas house, carefully scanning the numbers of the houses as they went. They found one at last before which they halted. The Captain searched in his pocket and drew forth the baby's letter to Santa Claus, and they examined the number under the gas lamp. Yes, that was right. The door was open, and they went right through to the rear.

Up in the third story three little noses were flattened against the window pane, and three childish mouths were breathing peep-holes through which to keep a lookout for the expected Santa Claus. It was cold, for there was no fire in the room, but in their fever of excitement the children didn't mind that. They were bestowing all their attention upon keeping the peep-holes open.

"Do you think he will come?" asked the oldest boy—there were two boys and a girl—of Kate.

"Yes, he will. I know he will come. Papa said so," said the child in a tone of conviction.

"I'se so hungry, and I want my sheep," said Baby Will.

"Wait and I'll tell you of the wolf," said his sister, and she took him on her lap. She had barely started when there were steps on the stairs and a tap on the door. Before the half-frightened children could answer it was pushed open. Two men stood on the threshold. One wore a big fur overcoat. The baby looked at him in wide-eyed wonder.

"Is you Santa Claus?" he asked.

"Yes, my little man, and are you Baby Will?" said a voice that was singularly different from the harsh one Baby Will's father had heard so recently in the Captain's office, and yet very like it.

"See. This is for you, I guess," and out of the big roomy pocket came the woolly sheep and baa-ed right off as if it were his own pasture in which he was at home. And well might any sheep be content nestling at a baby heart so brimful of happiness as little Will's was then, child of a thief though he was.

"Papa spoke for it, and he spoke for Kate, too, and I guess for everybody," said the bogus Santa Claus, "and it is all right. My sled will be here in a minute. Now we will just get to work and make ready for him. All help!"

The Sergeant behind the desk in the Detective Office might have had a fit had he been able to witness the goings-on in that rear tenement in the next hour; and then again he might not. There is no telling about those Sergeants. The way that poor flat laid itself out of a sudden was fairly staggering. It was not only that a fire was made and that the pantry filled up in the most extraordinary manner; but a real Christmas tree sprang up, out of the floor, as it were, and was found to be all besprinkled with gold and stars and cornucopias with sugarplums. From the top of it,

LITTLE WILL'S MESSAGE

which was not higher than Santa Claus could easily reach, because the ceiling was low, a marvellous doll, with real hair and with eyes that could open and shut, looked down with arms wide open to take Kate to its soft wax heart. Under the branches of the tree browsed every animal that went into and came out of Noah's Ark, and there were glorious games of Messenger Boy and Three Bad Bears, and honey-cakes and candy apples, and a little yellow-bird in a cage, and what not? It was glorious. And when the tea-kettle began to sing, skilfully manipulated by Santa Claus's assistant, who nominally was known in Mulberry Street as Detective Sergeant Murphy, it was just too lovely for anything. The baby's eyes grew wider and wider, and Kate's were shining with happiness, when in the midst of it all she suddenly stopped and said:—

"But where is papa? Why don't he come?"

Santa Claus gave a little start at the sudden question, but pulled himself together right away.

"Why, yes," he said, "he must have got lost. Now you are all right we will just go and see if we can find him. Mrs. McCarthy here next door will help you keep the kettle boiling and the lights burning till we come back. Just let me hear that sheep baa once more. That's right! I bet we'll find papa." And out they went.

An hour later, while Mr. ——, the Magistrate, and his good wife were viewing with mock dismay the array of little stockings at their hearth in their fine up-town house, and talking of the adventure of Mrs. —— with the pickpocket, there came a ring at the door-bell and the Captain of the detectives was ushered in. What he told them I do not know, but this I do know, that when he went away the honorable Magistrate went with him, and his wife waved good-by to them from the stoop with wet eyes as they drove away in a carriage hastily ordered up from a livery stable. While they drove down town, the Magistrate's wife went up to the nursery and hugged her sleeping little ones, one after the other, and tear-drops fell upon their warm cheeks that had wiped out the guilt of more than one sinner before, and the children smiled in their sleep. They say among the simple-minded folk of far-away Denmark that then they see angels in their dreams.

The carriage stopped in Mulberry Street, in front of Police Headquarters, and there was great scurrying among the reporters, for now they were sure of their "case." But no "prominent citizen" came out, made free by the Magistrate, who opened court in the Captain's office. Only a rough-looking man with a flushed face, whom no one knew, and who stopped on the corner and looked back as one in a dream and then went east, the way the Captain and his man had gone on their expedition personating no less exalted a personage than Santa Claus himself.

That night there was Christmas, indeed, in the rear tenement "near the gas house," for papa had come home just in time to share in its cheer. And there was no one who did it with a better will, for the Christmas evening that began so badly was the luckiest night in his life. He had the promise of a job on the morrow in his pocket, along with something to keep the wolf from the door in the holidays. His hard days were over, and he was at last to have his chance to live an honest life. And it was the baby's letter to Santa Claus and the baa sheep that did it all, with the able assistance of the Captain and the Sergeant. Don't let us forget the Sergeant.

THE BURGOMASTER'S CHRISTMAS

The burgomaster was in a bad humor. The smoke from his long pipe, which ordinarily rose in leisurely meditative rings signaling official calm and fair weather, came to-day in short, angry puffs as he tossed his mail impatiently about on the desk. A reprimand from headquarters, where they knew about as much of a burgomaster's actual work as he of the prime minister's! Less. Those bureaucrats never came in touch with real things. He smiled a little grimly as he thought that that was what his own people had said of him when twenty years before he had come from the capital to the little provincial town with his mind firmly made up to many things which—well, a man grows older and wiser. Life has its lessons for men, though it pass by the red tape in department bureaus. That never changes. His people and he, now—The stern wrinkle in the furrowed forehead relaxed, and he leaned back in his chair, blowing a long, contented ring, which brought a sigh of relief from the old clerk in the outer office. The skies were clearing.

In truth, despite his habitual sternness of manner, there was no more beloved man in the town of Hammel than the burgomaster. His kindness of heart was proverbial. The law had in him a faithful executor; the staff of office was no willow wand in his hand to bend to every wind that blew. To the evil-doer he was a hard master, but many were the stories that were whispered of how, having sent a thief to jail, he had taken care of his wife and children, who were not to blame. In fact, word had come from more than one distant town of how this or that ne'er-do-well, after squaring himself with the law in Burgomaster Brent's jurisdiction, had made a new start, helped somehow where he might have expected frowns and suspicion. But of this, Hammel tongues were careful not to wag within that official's hearing. Those things were his secret, if, indeed,—the matrons wagged their heads knowingly,—they were not his wife's, the burgomasterinde's; and so they were to stay.

Whether something of all this had come to smooth the burgomaster's brow or not, it was not for long. There was a tap on the door, and, in answer to his brisk "Come in," there entered Jens, the forester, with a swarthy, sullen-looking prisoner. Jens saluted and stood, cap in hand.

"Black Hans," he said briefly. "We took him last night in the meadow brake with a young roe."

The burgomaster's face grew cold and stern. Black Hans was an old offender. As a magistrate the burgomaster had given him a chance twice, but he was a confirmed poacher, who would rather lie out in the woods through a cold winter's night on the chance of getting a deer, and of getting into jail, too, than work a day at good wages, clever blacksmith though he was. Now he had been caught red-handed, and would be made to suffer for it. The burgomaster bent lowering brows upon the prisoner.

"You couldn't keep from stealing the count's deer, not even at Christmas," he said harshly.

The poacher looked up. Rough as he was, he was not a bad-looking fellow. The free, if lawless, life he led was in his face and bearing.

"The deer is wild. They're for the man as can take 'em, if the count do claim 'em," he said doggedly, and halted, as with a sudden thought. Something had entered with him and the forester, and was even then filling the room with a suggestion of good cheer to come. It was the smell of the Yule goose roasting in the burgomaster's kitchen. Black Hans looked straight into the eye of his inquisitor.

"I didn't have none—for me young ones," he added. It was not said defiantly, but as a mere statement of fact.

An angry reply rose to the official's lip, but he checked himself.

"Take him to the lock-up," he ordered shortly, and the forester went out with his charge.

The burgomaster heard the outer door close behind them, and turned wearily to his mail. The count had been greatly wrought up over the depredations of Black Hans and his kind, and would insist on an example being made of him. Bad blood always came of these cases, for the game law was not well thought of in the land in these democratic days. There lingered yet resentfully the recollection of the days not so long since when to take "the king's deer" brought a man to the block, or to the treadmill for life. And the family of this fellow Black Hans, what was to become of them? The burgomaster's gaze wandered abstractedly over the envelop he was opening and rested on an unfamiliar stamp. He held it up and took a closer look. Oh, yes; the new Christmas stamp. He knew it well enough, with its design of the great sanatorium for tubercular children that had been built out of the proceeds of other years' sales. It was a pretty picture, and a worthy cause. In all Denmark there was none that so laid hold of the popular fancy. It was the word "Yule," with its magic, that did it. There was no other inscription on the stamp, and none was needed.

As his glance dwelt upon it, a curious change came over the picture. It was no longer the great white house that he saw, with its many bright lights, but a wretched hut, with a crooked chimney, and rags stopping a broken pane in its only window. The dull glow of a tallow dip struggled through the grime that lay thick upon the unbroken panes. Against one the face of a child was pressed, a poor, pinched face that spoke of cold and hunger and weary waiting for some one who was always late. Something that was very much like real pain made the burgomaster wince as the words of Black Hans came back to him, "I didn't have none—for me young ones."

He shook his head impatiently. Why, then, did he not work for them, instead of laying it up against his betters?

The sober little face at the window kept looking out into the night, straight past the burgomaster, as if he were not there. How many of them in that hut? Seven, eight, nine, the burgomaster counted mentally; or was it ten ragged, underfed little ones, with the careworn mother who slaved from sunrise till night for them and her rascal husband? That child Annie who limped so pitifully, the district physician had told him that very morning, had tuberculosis of the hip-joint, and it was killing her slowly. Poor child! Surely this was she at the window. Her face looked pinched and small; yet she must be nearly eleven.

Eleven! The letter dropped unopened from the burgomaster's hand. That would have been the age of their own little girl had she lived. His pipe went out and grew cold; his thoughts were far away. They were travelling slowly back over a road he had shunned these many years, until he had almost lost the trail. His little Gertrude, their only child, a happy, winsome elf had filled the house with sunshine and laughter until in one brief month her life had gone out like the flame of a candle and left them alone! Since then they had been a lonesome couple. Tenderly attached to each other, but both silent, reserved people, husband and wife had locked their grief in their own hearts and tried to live it down.

Had they? He could even then see his wife at her work in the room across the yard. As she bent over her knitting, he noticed a little stoop which he had not seen before; and surely her hair was turning gray at the temples. His had long been so. They were growing old in their childless home. With a sudden pang there came to him a realization of the selfishness of his grief, which had shut her out of it. Christmas eve! What a happy time they used to have together in the old days around the tree! Even now he could hear the glad voices of children from the grocer's across the street, where they were making ready for theirs. In their house there had not been one since—since their Gertrude left them. There was Jens, the forester, carrying in a Christmas tree over there even now—Jens who had caught Black Hans. What sort of Christmas would they keep in his hut, with the father locked up, sure of a heavy fine, which meant a long time in jail, since he had no money to settle with?

The childish face with the grave eyes was at the window again, keeping its dismal watch. Eleven years! His mind went back, swiftly this time, over the freshly broken road to the days when the tree was lighted in their home on Christmas Eve. Of all the nights in the year, it had been the loneliest since, with just the two of them alone at the table, growing old.

A flood of tenderness swept over the burgomaster, and with it came a sudden resolve. It was not yet too late. He rose and slammed the desk down hard, leaving the rest of his mail unopened. Three o'clock! Almost time to light the candles, and this night he would light them himself. Yes, he would. He tapped on the window and beckoned to Jens, who was coming out of the grocery store. In the vestibule they held a brief whispered consultation that concluded with the warning, "and don't you tell my wife." The old clerk heard it and gave a start. What secret did the burgomaster have from the burgomasterinde which Jens, the forester, might share? But he remembered the day, in time, and bestowed upon himself a knowing wink. He, too, had his secrets.

Jens was less quick-witted. He offered some objection apparently, but it was promptly overruled by the burgomaster, who pushed him out with a friendly but decisive nod and bade him be gone.

"Very little ones—two, mind. And don't let her see."

Whereupon the burgomaster put on his overcoat and went out, too.

Before the church bells rang in the holy eve, all the gossips in town were busy with the report that the burgomaster had been buying enough Christmas toys and candles to stock an orphan asylum. What had come over the man? Five dolls, counted the toy-shop woman, with eyes that grew wide in the telling—five! And they alone, the two of them, in the big house with never a Christmas tree there that any one could remember! It must be that they were expecting company.

Nothing was further from the mind of the burgomasterinde as she went along with her preparations for the holiday. It had been a lonesome day with her, for all she had tried to fill it with housewifely tasks. Christmas eve always was. Now, as she sat with her knitting, her thoughts dwelt upon the days long gone when it had meant something to them; when a child's laughter had thrilled her mother heart. To her it was no unfamiliar road she was travelling. The memory of her child, which her husband had tried to shut out of his life lest it unman him for his work, she had cherished in her heart, and all life's burdens had been lightened and sweetened by it. Her one grief was that this of all things she could not share with him. No one ever heard her speak Gertrude's name, but there was sometimes a wistful look in her face which caused the burgomaster vague alarm, and once or twice had led to grave conferences with the family practitioner about Mrs. Brent's health. The old doctor, who was also the family friend, shook his head. The burgomasterinde was a well woman; his pills were not needed. Once he had hinted that her loss—but the burgomaster had interrupted him hastily. She would get over that, if indeed she had not quite forgotten; to stir it up would do no good. And the doctor, who was wise in other ways than those of his books, dropped the subject.

The burgomasterinde had seen Black Hans brought in in charge of Jens, and understood what the trouble was. As he was led away to the jail, her woman's heart yearned for his children. She knew them well. The town gossips were right: the path to the poacher's hut her familiar feet had found oftener than her stern husband guessed. The want and neglect in that wretched home stirred her to pity; but more than that it was the little crippled girl who drew her with the memory of her own. She had overheard the doctor telling her husband that there was no help for her

THE BURGOMASTER'S CHRISTMAS

where she was, and all day her mind had been busy with half-formed plans to get her away to the great seashore hospital where such cripples were made whole, if there was any help for them. Now, as she passed them in review, with the picture of Black Hans behind the bars for their background, a purpose grew up in her mind and took shape. They should not starve and be cold on Christmas eve, if their father *was* in jail. She would make Christmas for them herself. And hard upon the heels of this resolve trod a thought that made her drop her knitting and gaze long and musingly across the yard to the window at which her husband sat buried in his mail.

The burgomaster's face was turned from her. She could not see that he held in his hand the very letter with the Christmas stamp that had stirred unwonted thoughts within him; but she knew the furrow that had grown in the years of lonely longing. She had watched it deepen, and he had not deceived her, but she had vainly sought a way out. All at once she knew the way. They would keep Christmas again as of old, the two—nay, the three of them together. With a quick smile that had yet in it a shadow of fright, she went about carrying out her purpose.

So it befell that when Jens, the forester, was making off for the woods where the Christmas trees grew, shaking his head at the burgomaster's queer commission, the voice of the burgomasterinde called him back to the kitchen door, and he received the second and the greater shock of the day.

"Get two wee ones," she wound up her directions, "and bring them here to the back door. Don't tell my husband, and be sure he does not see."

Jens stared. "But the burgomaster—" he began. She stopped him.

"No matter about the burgomaster," she said briskly. "Only don't let him know. Bring them here as soon as it is dark."

And Jens departed, shaking his head in hopeless bewilderment.

The early winter twilight had fallen when he returned with two green bundles, one of which by dint of much strategy he smuggled into the front office without the burgomasterinde seeing him, while he delivered the other at the back door without the burgomaster being the wiser, this being made easier by the fact that the latter had not yet returned from his visit to the shops. When, a little while later he came home, tiptoeing in like a guilty Santa Claus on his early evening rounds, he shut himself in alone.

Profound quiet reigned in the official residence for a full hour after dark. In both wings of the house the shutters were closed tight. In one the burgomasterinde was presumably busy with her household duties; in the other the burgomaster was occupied with a task that would have made the old clerk doubt the evidence of his eyes had he himself not been at that moment engaged in the same identical business at his own home. Two small Christmas trees stood upon the table, from which law books and legal papers had been cleared with an unceremonious haste that had left them in an undignified heap on the floor. The burgomaster between them was fixing colored wax candles, cornucopias, and paper dolls in their branches. He eyed a bag of oranges ruefully. They were too heavy for the little trees, but then they would do to bank about the roots. To be sure, they had left these behind in the woods, but the fact was not apparent: each little tree was planted in a huge flower-pot, as Jens had received his orders, just as if it had grown there.

One brief moment the burgomaster paused in his absurd task. It was when he had put the last candle in place that something occurred to him which made him stand awhile in deep thought, gazing fixedly at the trees. Then he went to his desk, and from a back drawer, seldom used, took out something that shone like silver in the light. Perhaps it was that which made him screen his eyes with his hand when he saw it. It was a little silver star, such as many a Christmas tree bore at its top that night to tell the children of the Star of Bethlehem. The burgomaster sat and looked at it while the furrow grew deeper in his forehead; then he put it back gently into its envelop and closed the desk.

It was nearly time for dinner when he straightened up and heaved a sigh of contentment. The candles on one of the little trees were lighted, and all was ready.

"If only," he said uncertainly—"if only she is not in now." Could some good fairy have given him second sight to pierce the walls between his office and his wife's room, what he saw there would certainly have made him believe he had taken leave of his senses. Jens had just gone out with one Christmas tree, all hung with children's toys. On the table stood the other in its pot, a vision of beauty. The mistress of the house sat before it with a little box in her lap from which she took one cherished trinket after another, last of all a silvery angel with folded wings. A tear fell upon it as she set it in the tree, but she wiped this away and stood back, surveying her work with happy eyes. It *was* beautiful.

"I wonder where Jonas is. I haven't heard his step for an hour." She listened at the door. All was quiet. "I will just carry it over and surprise him when he comes in." And she went out into the hall with her shining burden.

At that precise moment the door of the office was opened, and the burgomaster came out, carrying his Christmas tree. They met upon the landing. For a full minute they stood looking at each other in stunned silence. It was the burgomaster who broke it.

"You were so lonely," he said huskily, "and I thought of our Gertrude."

She put down her tree, and went to him.

"Look, Jonas," she said, with her head on his shoulder, and pointed where it stood. He saw through blurring tears the child's precious belongings from her last Christmas,—their last Christmas,—and he bent down and kissed her.

"I know," he said simply; "it was Black Hans' little Annie. See!" He drew her into his office, "I made one for her. Jens shall take it over."

She hid her face on his breast. "He just went with one from me," she sobbed, struggling between laughter and tears; and as he started, she hugged him close. "But we need this one. I tell you, Jonas, what we will do: we will send it to Black Hans in the jail."

And even so it came to pass. To Jens's final and utter stupefaction, he was bidden to carry the fourth and last of the trees to the lock-up, where it cheered Black Hans that Christmas eve. It was noticed both by the turnkey and by the poacher that it bore a bright silver star at the top, but neither could know that it was to be a star of hope indeed for little Annie and her dark home. For so it had been settled between the burgomaster and his wife, as they pinned it on together and wished each other a right Merry Christmas, with many, many more to come, that happy night.

Copyright © 2022 by Alicia Editions
Cover and interior design: Canva.com; Alicia Ed.
Editor's Notes: A few typographical errors have been corrected.
All rights reserved.
No part of this book may be reproduced in any form or by any electronic or mechanical means, including information storage and retrieval systems, without written permission from the author, except for the use of brief quotations in a book review.

www.ingramcontent.com/pod-product-compliance
Lightning Source LLC
LaVergne TN
LVHW032012070526
838202LV00059B/6422